Fueling God's Mission with Prayer

Dave "the Prayer Guy" Roderick

ISBN 979-8-89345-912-8 (paperback)
ISBN 979-8-89345-926-5 (digital)

Copyright © 2024 by Dave "the Prayer Guy" Roderick

All rights reserved. No part of this publication may be reproduced, distributed, or transmitted in any form or by any means, including photocopying, recording, or other electronic or mechanical methods without the prior written permission of the publisher. For permission requests, solicit the publisher via the address below.

Christian Faith Publishing
832 Park Avenue
Meadville, PA 16335
www.christianfaithpublishing.com

Scripture taken from THE HOLY BIBLE, NEW INTERNATIONAL VERSION®. Copyright© 1973, 1978, 1984, 2011 by Biblica, Inc.™. Used by permission of Zondervan

Printed in the United States of America

Contents

Acknowledgment v
Foreword..vii
Introduction..ix
Chapter 1: My Journey 1
Chapter 2: Understand God's Mission 6
Chapter 3: Prayer That God Always Answers 17
Chapter 4: Prayer in All Its Fullness 28
Chapter 5: Praying the Scriptures.......................43
Chapter 6: Spiritual Warfare 53
Chapter 7: Trusting God as an Act of Prayer 60
Chapter 8: Leaders in the Church 66
Chapter 9: Spiritual Formation and
　　　　　 God's Mission 76
Chapter 10: The Family and God's Mission 84
Chapter 11: The Mission in Business and
　　　　　 With Money 92
Chapter 12: Praying for Government Leaders 100
Conclusion...113

Acknowledgment

The idea for this book has been brewing in me for many years. It has been a journey since becoming born-again in October of 1994. The first person I want to thank is Yahweh. He has saved me and given me this vision of fueling his mission with prayer. Thank you, Yahweh, for everything you have done and will do.

I thank my wife, Tina, who has supported me as I develop a prayer-based ministry. She has read my fiction stories, and I value her feedback. She is my life partner and the most important person on earth to me.

Thank you to the many people who have prayed with me over the years. I especially thank Paul Basko (I will look you up when I get to heaven and share with you how God worked in me to write this book), who prayer-walked with me many times in Sanford, Maine. I will go into more detail later. Thank you to all the prayer partners I've had over the years.

I love how God has placed people in my life. I waited years to have a prayer ministry position in my church. Pastor Scott Benner first allowed me to have a prayer-based ministry in a church. Thank you, Scott! Later, as I worked for Marketplace Chaplains, part-time, I met Mark Soone, who took the time to read the manuscript. Thank you, Mark! Also, thank you for trusting me to be the prayer coordinator at the River Church.

Thank you to my supervisors at InterVarsity, who realized that prayer is my wheelhouse. Will Trusedell and John Haslam for allowing me to develop and think about prayer as a base ministry.

After InterVarsity, I volunteered in a ministry called Christian Revelation. Thank you, Randy Brown, for allowing me to try a few things and develop my thoughts of praying more missionally.

Thank you to those who partner with me in Main Prayer Strategy, Ron and Jon. Thanks for your support as I gather the bride of Christ for prayer.

Foreword

I first met Dave in 2022 through "Market Place Chaplains," a super cool organization with which we both continue to partner in Bangor, Maine. We quickly hit it off, and it has been an honor to serve as his pastor and, even better, as his friend for the past two years. Dave serves as the prayer coordinator at The River Church in Bangor. He is the Coordinator of the Penobscot County branch of "Main Prayer Strategy," where Dave pours himself into uniting believers, churches, and pastors into prayer partnerships for our communities.

Like very few people you will meet, Dave has a passion for God and for communing with Him in prayer. In this book, Dave shares some of his own journey in Christ, his passion for God and prayer, and his utter belief that our prayers are "Fuel for God's mission."

What if prayer is not simply the least that we can do but rather the most and best that we can do? What if we truly lived, believed, and prayed like God wanted to spend time with us? What if we truly lived, believed, and prayed like God was willing and desiring to transform our lives, community, and world? What if we truly believed that God was waiting for men and women who would seek His face to pour His kingdom blessing out upon our lives, families, churches, and neighbors? Jesus said, "Ask, and it will be given to you; seek, and you will find; knock, and the door will be opened. For everyone who asks receives; the one who seeks finds; and to the one who knocks, the door will be opened" (Matthew 7:7-8). What would happen if the people of God lived, believed, and prayed, asking and trusting that He is a GREAT God, and He desires to do Great things to us, through us and all around us? I think He would turn our world upside down!

So, if you are hungry and thirsty to see the power of God come alive in your life, your family, your church, and your world find a quiet and comfortable spot to settle into as you join Dave on this journey of drawing closer to God, and seeking His face and trusting and expecting His glorious miracles to follow. I trust that you will be blessed by reading and listening to Dave's heart on these pages, and I trust that we will all be transformed, as well as the world around us, as we seek God's face together.

Mark Soone
Pastor, River Church in Bangor, Maine

Introduction

I love prayer. There is nothing more that I want to do! I also love to talk and teach about prayer. And I especially love praying with other people. I even like praying about prayer. The topic I pray for the most is God's mission. This book flows from that love to teach what it means to pray missionally. Prayer is the fuel for God's mission, and the ministry that God gave me is to fuel God's mission and to help others.

My love for prayer came to life when I asked to join the prayer team for InterVarsity's orientation for new staff out in Madison, Wisconsin. The plan was simple. After breakfast, we would join the Bible study time and then go to the prayer room. We would review their schedule and pray for the staff. Then it would be a break for us. Then during their free time, we were available to pray for anyone that requested it.

I must admit that I was disappointed when there wasn't a staff looking for prayer during the afternoon. I would have to find something to be praying for as I waited. I did a lot of prayer-walking in Madison, Wisconsin. I would remain in the prayer room and pray for the new staff. The best part of the week was all that time for prayer.

Toward the end of orientation, the new staff was to spend time reflecting on the week. The rest of the prayer team rested while I prayed for the staff because I couldn't get enough, and I wanted those staff to be ready. I walked the city streets because the staff spread out. I probably won't know how God answered those prayers this side of heaven, but I know he did. I know I have been part of all the college campuses that those staff represented and what God did.

The idea of missional prayer developed over the last few years. God showed me this through his Word, books written by other believers, and listening to God through his still, small voice and conversations with others. After a while, I decided to go on this journey to write. It helped me organize my thoughts.

I started writing again in the fall/winter of 2020 and 2021. At first, it was writing a combination of stories and missional prayer. I took a break from writing the book on missional prayer and focused on my fictional stories. In the meantime, I published my first story: *They Came to Proclaim.*

There is some teaching on prayer woven into *They Came to Proclaim.* I didn't realize it until a friend read the manuscript. I took what he said to heart and expanded many parts with prayer. I hope readers will better understand prayer and how God can work in a story format.

Grab your favorite beverage and snack, and start reading. I pray that this book will help shape your prayers into a missional focus and that you will fuel God's mission with prayer. It is God's mission. We are called to partner with him. Let's be praying early and often.

Chapter 1

My Journey

Prayer is my lifeline. It has been since I decided to follow Jesus as a freshman at the University of Maine. In September of 1994, I entered the campus and the fellowship of InterVarsity as a seeker. By October, I decided to be a disciple of Christ. Instantly, I spent my college years inviting others to pray with me. I also was a regular at InterVarsity's daily prayer meeting.

I was introduced to prayer-walking in college. Simply stated, prayer walking is praying while you are walking. The weather was perfect for my first-time prayer walk—not hot, and not cold. While we walked, we talked to each other and God as if he was there with us in the flesh. We made stops to pray, and one stop sticks out to me. We stopped outside Bennett Hall to pray for professors. I prayed for my Astronomy 101 professor to realize that God is the Creator and involved in more than just the Big Bang.

I don't know how God answered that prayer. It is the first time I have ever prayed for something I believe God asked me to pray, but I didn't realize it at first. It was the start of my learning how to pray missionally. God is on a mission to save people. I was praying for this professor to know God, a prayer I would be surprised that God didn't answer in the affirmative. It was also the first time I could look back to that I was joining God in his mission.

I did more prayer walks when I moved to Springvale, Maine. I met weekly with a friend and suggested that we prayer-walk monthly. We would meet near the town sections that we wouldn't want to be at night. Our walks combined talking to God and talking to each other. Whatever we walked past, we would pray for it. We prayed for people, churches, playgrounds, schools, etc. I missed these prayer walks because not only did I grow closer to God but I also got to know my friend more.

It wasn't long before I started prayer-walking on my own at other times. This was when I began to hear God's voice. I started reading all kinds of books on prayer because I wanted to learn more and know the voice of God. If there was a prayer meeting I could attend, I was there. I could pray alone, but I felt more alive praying with others.

Later I felt a calling to work for InterVarsity Christian Fellowship. The application process was long, and I needed a lot of prayers before. And after submitting the application, I prayed. After the interview, I went for a prayer walk to clear my head and get God's directions. It was a tough interview. I prayed for God to show me if I should accept the position. God provided the answer the next day.

I'm thankful I worked for InterVarsity because I learned about vocational ministry. Unfortunately, I never got funding to be full-time, and I left the ministry after six years. I did daily prayer walks on campus, sometimes with students and by myself. Building that time into my work time during the week was excellent.

For the last two years, I was the payer coordinator for Northern New England, my favorite position with InterVarsity. I would go to the campuses around Northern New England and either pray or teach about prayer from the Bible, and sometimes it was both. I had found my stride. Unfortunately, after two years as the prayer coordinator, I was no longer with InterVarsity.

The summer of 2015 was the start of the most challenging summer of my life. I didn't know what I wanted to do for full-time work. I still had my part-time job, and I was picking up hours that were crazy: doubles on both Mondays and Fridays, and 7:00 a.m. to 3:00 p.m. or 3:00 p.m. to 11:00 p.m. on Saturday. I applied, accepted offers, changed my mind, and even worked a job for only two weeks, just wanting it to end. Finally, I did land a Tuesday through Saturday 7:00 a.m. to 3:00 p.m. job.

That summer also saw me praying and walking a lot. Since I had every Tuesday, Wednesday, and Thursday off, I decided to prayer walk every street in Old Town, Maine. I didn't reach that goal, but I walked and prayed for many roads, houses, schools, and people. Sometimes I went alone, and other times

I prayed and walked with others. The times praying for others were life-giving.

Also, that summer, I started helping with a ministry that uses music called Christian Revelation. The ministry wanted revival, and prayer was a big part of it. After a few years of involvement, I moved on because I wanted to focus more on prayer. At the same time, I learned about the Main Prayer Strategy and joined them as the Penobscot County (Maine) coordinator back in 2019. I enjoy it because I'm leading prayer, talking about prayer, and praying with others for God to do amazing things.

Joining the Main Prayer Strategy is an interesting story. At first, I wasn't sure I wanted to join. It appeared then that MPS was more about leaders praying than the church praying. I decided to go to the first MPS gathering in the Greater Bangor, Maine area. It was mostly a vision-casting night, but we prayed. Everyone had the opportunity to pray. I loved it. I was the only one standing when they asked if anyone was interested in being the coordinator for that area.

Along the way, I learned about God's mission. I have read books about how the Bible is one story of God's plan for redemption. I took an Old Testament survey class and, later, a New Testament class. As I learned about God's mission, I've become convinced that it should be the focus of my prayers. This book is what I believe God has been teaching me over the years and how he wants me to help lead his church.

FUELING GOD'S MISSION WITH PRAYER

I write about my journey because we are all on a journey. Where you are now in life is not an accident. God is working in your life. My prayer for sharing this is to encourage you to reflect on where you have been with God and see how he has been forming. Embrace the struggles because they are shaping you. Remember that Romans 8:28 says, "And we know that in all things God works for the good of those who love him, who have been called to his purpose."

Chapter 2

Understand God's Mission

Over the years, I have enjoyed and read many books about how the Bible is one story from Genesis to Revelation. The first book I read was the *Road to Emmaus* by John R. Cross. That was read shortly after I graduated from college. It was read and discussed as part of a Sunday school. Later, I read it to my son when he was old enough to understand.

While working with InterVarsity, I was part of a Sunday school class, reading the book *God's Big Story* by Vaughan Roberts. I ate it up! It was very similar to the Road to Emmaus. It was the same information but explained in a different format. That class was the week's highlight every week until we finished the book.

Later on, the traveling team came to UMaine. This team travels to secular universities and colleges to talk about the one story of God from Genesis to Revelation. I invited them to come to speak to the college students in InterVarsity and asked the other campus ministry groups to join us. That night, I was again ministered to and reminded of God's story of redemption.

One of the highlights of my Christian walk is taking the Old Testament and New Testament survey courses. To be frank, I knew I would enjoy the Old Testament survey because I enjoy the stories of the Old Testament. When I took the New Testament survey course, I enjoyed that just as much because it was about Jesus as the solution to the problem of sin in the world. The New Testament is the fulfillment of the Old Testament.

These two courses used the acronym CASKET EMPTY. CASKET is for Creation, Abraham, Sinai, Kings, Exile, and Temple. At the same time, EMPTY is Expectations, Messiah, Pentecost, Teachings, and Yet to come. This is a great tool to help place a story from the Bible in the context of God's mission and story. I read the Old Testament study for CASKET EMPTY, which was great. I haven't read the New Testament one yet, but it has to be based on the class.

I joined a community life group, and we read *The God Who Is There* by D. A. Carson. The author walked us through how God has revealed himself in Scripture. As he shares, I'm amazed once again how I'm reminded that we have turned our backs on God, yet he still loves and is reaching out to us. This is another book I highly recommend all Christians read. Once again, it is the story of the Bible.

My church, United Baptist in Old Town, Maine, challenged us to read the *Story*. Max Lucado and Randy Alcove compile this. They put together passages in the Bible in chronological order so the Bible reads like a novel. On Sunday mornings, the pastors preached from a passage in one of the chapters.

Why do I share all this? I firmly believe that if you want to be praying for God's mission, you need to understand God's mission. As I'm sure you have heard before, God will never contradict his Word, the Bible. As I study it, I'm amazed at how it all worked together to express God's love for us and what he is doing to redeem his creation.

My challenge to you is, don't stop studying the Bible! There are so many resources out there that are written well and will teach you about God's mission. If you don't know where to start, I recommend any I have written here. You can also talk to your pastor, who has probably read one or two and can recommend one. Your pastor will know of other resources that I'm not aware of.

I would like to discuss God's mission to understand it. I will have each section titled with a Bible passage that is important to understand God's mission. I suggest that you read over the passage with God. What I mean by that is to realize that God will speak to you and highlight things he hasn't highlighted before. Again, the more you understand God's mission, the better you can share it and, more importantly, pray for it.

The Problem

Genesis 1 and 2 are about the creation of the world. Right in the beginning, we learn that God exists and is the Creator. The Bible doesn't give proof that God exists; it only tells us. We also understand that we are made in the image of God. Since God is the creator and we are his creation, it goes without saying that God is sovereign. The critical thing to remember here is that God made the world perfect.

Genesis 3 is about the problem of sin entering the world. Adam sinned by not stopping Eve from eating the fruit from the only tree God commanded them not to eat from. Eve sinned by eating the fruit and offering it to Adam. They both sinned by rejecting God's plan. Isn't that the case with us today? We leave God's design. We decided that our ways were better than God's. There is an inherent problem in all of us to turn our backs on God.

Then separation happens; separation from God. There is a break from each other. Adam blames Eve, and then Eve blames the serpent. It is difficult to realize that we are all part of the problem. I discussed sin at an InterVarsity conference and used archery to explain that sin is missing the mark. Sin in archery is not hitting the bull's-eye. Anything outside of God's design is a sin.

Before this chapter ends, God hints at the solution. That someone was coming to fix the problem. I love that! It didn't take God long to say that he would fix this. Stop here for a moment. As soon as the problem enters the world, God is ready to work to fix it. Praise God! He doesn't want to leave us in our mess. God desires us to hit the bull's-eye all the time. I know we won't hit the bull's-eye this side of heaven, but I will share more about God's desire to hit it every time.

The following few chapters show how sin keeps getting worse. With each turn of the page, the problem gets worse. God shows his power by wiping away everyone in the flood of all time except one family (which shows God's great love). The story of the flood shows us God's judgment and grace. The opening chapters of Genesis are clear. There is a severe problem with the world: it is us. We have decided that we don't need God and live in an insulting way to the one who gave us life.

Throughout the Old Testament, God continues to explain more and more of the problem, how we missed the mark. The heroes of the Old Testament all have a sinful problem. Thankfully, the Old Testament does proclaim what the solution is. It starts with a man named Abram, whom God changed his name to Abraham.

Every step of the way, God uses circumstances to teach Israel that a savior is coming. Abraham was older when God finally came through on his promise of a son, Isaac. God also promised Abraham that he would have many descendants and that God would bless the world through him. One of those descendants would be the world's savior, the Messiah, the blessing God promised.

I wonder how Abraham must have felt when God promised him a son. On top of that, God promises his descendants would number the stars. My question for us is whether we believe God or question him. Abraham believed. Remember, he was human and part of the problem. God picked someone who was childless, a least likely person to work through. Abraham did try to help God with Hagar. God forgave him and still used him.

Later we have the story of the sacrifice of Isaac. Abraham trusted God to bring Isaac back or to give him another son. I love that God provided another sacrifice. At the right time, the angel of the Lord stopped him and provided the ram. This is an excellent picture of the death and resurrection of Jesus. Jesus is the lamb who provided for the sacrifice and returned so we could have a live Messiah. Isaac was saved.

The law from Moses not only allowed us to realize we are sinners but also pointed to God's plan to save the world. The Law had provisions for covering sin with sacrifices. Each sacrifice had to be perfect, pointing to a blameless redeemer. Leviticus is an excellent book that points to Jesus. When trying to read through the Bible, I know many people get discouraged when they hit this book. When I read it, I try to remember how it is trying to explain what it will do.

King David wanted to build a temple. God said, "No, David's son will build the temple." God also used this time to explain his plan once again.

God would make David's name great and establish his throne forever. One from David's line would sit on his throne for all time. Jesus is going to be that king.

As you read the prophets of the Old Testament, you see more and more of God's plan. The Messiah was coming; he was going to be our king and priest. I remember one story from one of the prophets. This prophet had a vision with both Joshua, the high priest, and Zerubbabel, the governor in David's royal line. In the vision, the priest was crowned. This speaks to how Jesus will be both king and priest. In summary, the Old Testament speaks to the problem and God's solution.

The Solution

While the Old Testament speaks to the problem in the world and the solution, the New Testament explains why Jesus is the solution. The Gospels give us the story of Jesus's life and ministry. Jesus is the solution because he offers the needed sacrifice and because it is the only way we can be transformed. This transformation is salvation. We are sinners that are saved by grace, and this grace is from Jesus.

I believe that salvation occurs when we trust Jesus to do what we can't do. There is a now, but not yet to this salvation. Jesus is there at every step of the way, transforming us. Let's be honest with those of us that are Christians: we still sin. Jesus is still at work in us daily, forming us into his image.

Every Christmas, I read Luke 2 to remind my family about the birth of Jesus. One thing that sticks out to me is the announcement from the angels. They tell us that Jesus is Christ the Lord or Messiah. The Messiah brings peace on earth, peace between God and man. I wish I were there to see the angels announcing the birth of Jesus. I love what the shepherds do next: they check out what the angels tell them.

In the Gospels, we read about the life, ministry, death, and resurrection of Jesus. I recommend reading the Gospels to understand what Jesus did on earth. I love that he picked twelve disciples to be Apostles, to do the work with him, and that he spent time getting to know them. Jesus not only spent time with the twelve but he also ate with sinners and tax collectors. He went to those who needed him.

The event I need to talk about is the cross. Throughout the Old Testament, God's people had a system of sacrifices. All of them point to Jesus dying on the cross. The best part in all this is that Jesus came back alive. Yes, he was dead and buried from Friday to Sunday, but he is alive now. I once had a friendly debate about which event was more important, the death of Jesus or the resurrection. Without death, we don't have the sacrifice to be cleansed of our sins. The resurrection tells us that God accepted the death, and we now have a savior alive and still at work.

In the Gospels, Jesus invites others to participate in his mission. He sends out the twelve and then the seventy to share about Jesus. At the end of

Matthew, he commands his disciples to go out into the world to make disciples, teaching them to obey. If you follow Jesus, you are part of this mission. We are his disciples scattered throughout the nations. We are part of this mission.

I will discuss this later, but I want to bring it up now. The Great Commission found in Matthew 28:18–20 speaks about helping people become disciples and then helping them to obey everything Jesus commands. This speaks to the mission of God to be about evangelism and discipleship. This is the mission we are called into.

Acts is about the start of the church. I love how it starts with Jesus telling them not to worry about times and events that are set by the Father but to go out and be witnesses. Luke writes that they start in Jerusalem and then move out to a broader area until they have reached the ends of the world. Compared to Jerusalem, we live at the ends of the earth. This is a command for us. Let's go out to be the church with Jesus.

I want to return to Acts 1:11–14 because it speaks to how the disciples returned to Jerusalem and prayed. They came together for the next ten days and prayed. Yes, during that time, they picked another disciple to replace Judas; but for me, that was a side note to what they were doing because even that was covered with prayer. The answer to their prayers was the Holy Spirit; once they had the Holy Spirit, they had the power to do the mission. The church has grown from these prayers. Your church can grow from your prayer and with the prayers of others.

Jesus promises to be with us through the Holy Spirit. He is working through us to share Christ with others. We need to be connected to him in prayer. John 15 tells us that Jesus is the vine and the Father is the gardener. It is good to spend time going back to him.

If you are a disciple of Jesus, this command is also for you. He calls all of us to do our part in advancing the kingdom of Christ. The vision for my life is to fuel God's mission with prayer. So I pray for those and myself to engage in sharing the Gospel and for disciples to grow to Christian maturity. Yes, prayer is vitally important, but so is getting out of the prayer closet and getting involved in the lives of others in hopes that they will become disciples. We are to do what we can to improve the world with God. Prayer and actions are required.

Why Understand His Mission

Praying for new disciples is a prayer that God loves to answer. It might take years or decades, but if we are faithful, God will answer those prayers and grow his church. When I'm going on prayer walks, God's mission is the focus of my prayer. When I pray for God to heal the sick and the injured, it is in light of his mission. I believe that God can use anything to save the lost. That is always my prayer. The more I understand his mission, the more my prayers can focus on God's heart and the prayers he desires to hear from me.

I also focus my prayers on believers to grow to maturity. If they are sick or injured, I will pray for them to be healed; but more importantly, I'm praying for them to grow to maturity. I pray for Christians to continue learning and growing in Jesus.

Over the years, one change in my prayers has shifted from praying for salvation to praying for more disciples and laborers for the Gospel. I don't want to leave new Christians at the altar of salvation, but I want to see them go out and bring others there. God isn't just looking for people to join him in heaven but also for people who will join him to improve the world.

Chapter 3
Prayer That God Always Answers

When I was growing up, I knew there was God. I'm thankful my mom brought me to church because it laid a foundation for God to work in my life when I went to college. When I was a kid, I would play church at home. I was the priest, and my toys were the congregation. I had a copy of the service order and followed the mass very well. (I grew up in the Roman Catholic Church.) But the teaching of Christ was limited to when I was in church and CCD, or Christian Catechism Development. When my sister went through confirmation, that is when I started to question religion.

You might be wondering what I mean by questioning religion. It didn't make sense that my sister used confirmation for a graduation ceremony. In other words, she had done her religious duty and was free to live as she chose. I saw confirmation as a declaration that the Catholic Church was your church.

If confirmation was only a graduation, I didn't want to be part of it. I asked that question repeatedly but didn't get a satisfying answer. This was the start of my seeking the truth.

I chose the University of Maine because it meant I could go away to college. I grew up in New Hampshire, and the two hours to Durham, New Hampshire, and UNH were too close for me. But the five-and-half hours were enough for me to feel like I had gotten away from home. Don't get me wrong, the home in New Hampshire was great. I had two loving parents, and one of them brought me to church; and that experience, as I said before, laid the foundation for what God had in store for me at UMaine.

I stepped onto the campus in Orono, Maine, in the fall of 1994 as a seeker of the truth. Little did I know that God was ready to meet me. I heard the gospel for the first time on Labor Day and rejected it because I felt I was only a potential notch in the belt of that person's brand of Christianity. I have since become friends with this man, knowing his heart was in the right place.

That same weekend I met students from InterVarsity, and they invited me into their group and showed me the love of Christ. Through their lives and answers to my questions, they delivered and told me that Jesus saves. That October, I became a Christian in my dorm room after the fall retreat.

I share this because Jesus does save, even at a secular university like the University of Maine. It's good to reflect on the events that led to you becoming a Christian. As we think about praying for God's mission, we need to remember that Jesus saves, and he wants to save. John 3:16 says, "God loves the world, so he sent his son to save it."

I know that I was prayed into the kingdom, starting with John 17, because Jesus prayed that people would believe because of the apostles' message. Think about it: the apostles shared Christ's message, and those who it was shared with shared the same message; and eventually, that message came to UMaine. I don't remember if any of my friends in college told me that they were praying for me as I moved from the world's kingdom to Jesus's kingdom, but I would be surprised if none of them did. Our campus staff also sent out his newsletter to his supporters, and he prayed. I believe that this is the prayer that God loves to answer.

Paul's Prayer Request

Paul in Colossians 4:2-4 says to "devote yourself to prayer." He asks for prayer for himself as he proclaims the gospel and that doors will be open. His prayer request is Gospel-centric, wanting the message to go forth. Indeed, that prayer, Jesus answered because Paul's ministry grew as he traveled to share the Gospel. After all, people prayed for it.

Since this prayer is in Scripture, it must be a prayer that God wants us to be praying. Of course, I'm not talking about praying for Paul, but praying for pastors, missionaries, and other ministry leaders.

Pray that they can proclaim the gospel clearly and that doors will be open. Don't just limit your prayers to the professionals but also pray for everyone that are Christian. We all need to be active in God's mission, and we need prayer. Pray for your friends who are Christians and yourself to clearly express the gospel and have opportunities to share their hope.

There are support ministries that need our prayers for God's kingdom. These people might not be upfront about sharing the message, but these behind-the-scenes people need our prayers as well. These are the ones who help with the church's technology, work in the church office, and are prayer warriors. We all need prayer to make sure our focus is on God and his mission.

A Suggested Prayer

In the past few years, I have learned of a prayer called "Pray for one." Bo Chancey developed this prayer in Manchester, New Hampshire (another reason New Hampshire is incredible). The idea behind this prayer is to pray daily that you will share the love of Christ with one person. I have a reminder on my phone to pray for one every day at 7:00 p.m. God has revealed someone to pray for specifically as I continue to pray for one. I ask God to allow me to share his love with this person daily.

For others, praying for one becomes a scavenger hunt of sorts. They go throughout their day looking for the opportunity God has given them. There have been times when I find myself in a situation helping someone, and I know it is God who has directed me. As you can see, this is one prayer that you can use to help you pray to fuel God's mission.

The Harvest

Many Christians, if not all, are familiar with the story of the woman at the well found in John 4. This is a great story of Jesus sharing who he is and why he came. Ultimately, the woman shares about Jesus with those who live near her.

At this point in the story, Jesus is talking to his disciples. He looks up and points to the crowd coming toward them. Jesus tells them that the harvest is ripe. In Matthew 9, he talks about praying for workers for the harvest. Instead of saying we should pray for those saved, he says to pray for harvesters. Let that sink in. Jesus doesn't command us to pray for salvation but for harvesters, those who live a life of mission.

I have read this passage many times, and it is only recently that this point hit me hard. I haven't stopped praying for people to become disciples, but I have started to pray that God will raise evangelists. I wonder if Jesus was saying, "If my people would just engage with sharing with others about me, people will be saved." Or, put another way, inviting others to experience life change with Jesus.

Praying for the Unsaved

When I first wrote this chapter, I didn't have this section. I was convinced that no passage of Scripture speaks to praying for people to be saved. Then Jesus showed me John 17. This is primarily a prayer for unity. Yes, the church needs unity, and I do pray for that unity in the mission of God. But Jesus prays for those of us who believe because of the message.

It hit me. Jesus was praying for his mission to go out. He was praying and knew that people like you and me would become Christians because of the apostles' message, and those who came after you and I are answers to Jesus's prayer. This is an example of praying for new believers or new disciples. Yes, pray for the harvesters and for people to decide to follow Jesus.

This is the second time I have brought up John 17. This was a critical passage to bring up again. If Jesus prayed this prayer, he must want it answered.

The Other Part of God's Mission

When I worked for InterVarsity, one of the things I liked about their mission was helping Christian students grow in their faith. We didn't want only to evangelize the lost and then leave them at the altar of salvation but to also bring them along to Christian maturity. I believe that is also part of God's mission, the growth of all current disciples. If we pray for God's mission, we need to understand. Let's look at a well-known Bible verse.

> Then Jesus came to them and said, "All authority in heaven and on earth has been given to me. Therefore go and make disciples of all nations, baptizing them in the name of the Father and of the Son and the Holy Spirit, and teaching them to obey everything I have commanded you. And surely I am with you always, to the very end of the age." (Matthew 28:18–20)

Praying for the Christian growth of others is another prayer that God loves to answer. The Great Commission in Matthew says to make disciples and then teach them to obey everything that Jesus taught. Do you see that order? People need Christ to follow everything he has commanded. We can do this prayer because Jesus has the authority to help people grow to Christian maturity. Pray for your friends to overcome sin. Pray for your friends to engage in God through the Word.

Let's go back to Acts 1:8 because it helps us understand how Jesus will be with us until the end of the age. The passage says, "But you will receive power when the Holy Spirit comes on you." Yes, there is more to the verse, but I want us to focus on the fact that the Holy Spirit will come to us. Jesus is with us through the Holy Spirit. Without the Holy Spirit, we will not have the power to do what we need to do. This is another reason why we need to pray.

Don't forget to pray for yourself. Your discipleship is essential to God and part of his mission. Pray to understand Scripture. Pray to overcome that sin in your life that you struggle with. Pray for opportunities to help fellow believers grow and share your faith with not-yet Christians.

Tension

There is tension with prayer. Jesus says in John 14:14, "You may ask for anything in my name, and I will do it." That is a big claim. And Jesus is up to the task. Let's be honest: sometimes we pray and God doesn't give us the answer we want. Do you remember the movie *God's Not Dead*? The professor tells a story of when he was a kid praying for his mom to be healed, and she died. Why didn't Jesus answer that prayer?

I won't answer that question because I don't know the answer. I can see some of you are mad at me. I'm okay with that. The purpose of the previous paragraph is to remind us that Jesus is not the cosmic vending machine in the sky. He will answer prayers in his ways. And the movie doesn't answer the question. I can speculate that maybe the professor needed to go through that to be ready to come to Jesus at the right time. That is only speculation.

FUELING GOD'S MISSION WITH PRAYER

Show of hands. Who has prayed and didn't get their desired answer? I bet it is all of us. One example from my life is when I worked for InterVarsity. I worked part-time because the funding wasn't there for full-time. I prayed and prayed that God would provide funding for full-time. Then after six years, he took InterVarsity away from me instead of giving full-time hours.

How do we reconcile this? There are things that we know for sure. God is sovereign; he isn't the tremendous cosmic vending machine in the sky that desires to give us gifts. Just like in the verse from James that says "we don't have because we didn't ask." Or the story of the persistent widow in Luke. I prayed a lot to be full-time with InterVarsity, and God didn't give it to me.

Some of you might think God has something better for me, and I agree. But this tension remains. Remember that God is the God who wants to give good gifts to the right person at the right time. That is a helpful thought. Sometimes God wants to provide what is best, and good is not always best. Don't get me wrong; God has answered prayers for me before. He has provided me with jobs and a new focus.

Remember, my discipleship journey is part of God's mission. Leaving InterVarsity hurt; it was work that I enjoyed and good work. Maybe it was best for me only for a time. God had some work to do for me, and leaving InterVarsity was part of it. I still pray for the college campus, but now the focus is on the general population in towns and cities. Jesus was giving me a larger vision for his mission, a larger vision for prayer.

The question we need to ask is, what does praying in Jesus's name mean? The name of Jesus means "to deliver or save." I have also heard it means "Yahweh saves." I wonder if praying Jesus's name means any prayers that help bring about God's kingdom. God can use all things to help people realize their need for him.

I believe God wants us to pray for more people to become disciples. He wants to answer that prayer and work in the lives of others. God's mission has a lot of needs, like people sharing the gospel and for hearts to be softened and ready to hear that God loves them and wants to save them. God will do whatever is needed to advance the kingdom, including answering a prayer with no or something different.

The same is true with us as believers in our path to Christian maturity. God will use anything that will grow you, including not answering a prayer how you want it. That shouldn't stop you from praying. Prayer needs to be more about spending time with God than what we can get from God.

I continue to reflect on my time with InterVarsity. I learned a lot about professional ministry. I use that reflection today as I volunteer for Main Prayer Strategy and am the church's prayer coordinator. God will continue to mold and shape me. He is preparing me for the following tasks he has for me. Those tasks could be when I'm in heaven or before I leave earth.

What is the prayer that God always wants to answer? His kingdom is advanced. In the following chapters, I will outline different ways that can look. Keep in mind that God will not always answer in the way you think God should answer it. As he is making disciples, he is also going to grow disciples. Trust his plan and keep on praying.

Answer to the Tension

The other night I was watching *Rudy*. My favorite line is the priest telling Rudy. I don't remember exactly what it is he said, but this is what I remember: "There is a God, and I'm not him." I love this line because it speaks to the truth that God is sovereign.

God has his reasons for doing what he is doing. Ultimately, it is about his mission and will. I don't know why God only had me part of InterVarsity for about six years, but I know he knows what he is doing. Looking back, I can see how God used me; when the time was over, it was over. Some of me still doesn't know exactly what I am doing. That is okay. I trust God.

A quick note about InterVarsity: God still uses it to bring students to himself. He is also still working through and in the staff and student leaders. I still pray for InterVarsity. My supervisor was correct: there was something better for me in God's mission.

What is the answer to this tension? It is simple: trust God. Spend time with his Word in prayer. Talk to and listen to him. And know that God has a plan and knows what he is doing.

Chapter 4

Prayer in All Its Fullness

In my mind, prayer is about spending time with God by sharing your concerns, requests, and joys and listening to him. To have prayer at its fullest will take time. The best way to explain this is to share a day I took just for prayer.

A Day Dedicated to Prayer

I was taking a prayer retreat in Gilford, New Hampshire. I chose that town because it was where I grew up. The year before, I decided to do the same thing in Sanford, Maine, where my development as a prayer warrior started. I believe that place is essential. It needs to be special to you in some way. A place where you know you can relax and get away. You might not be able to get away as I did, but there must be places near you where you can go to spend time with God there.

I didn't rush the day. Most days, most people get up early to get ready for work. Hopefully, a quiet time or devotion is part of the morning routine. On these mornings, there is a little rush. Time for prayer, exercise, breakfast, getting dressed, and finally, leaving for work. That morning, I didn't rush. There is something about taking your time that feels restful. I remember a teacher telling me that she gets up at the same time on her days off, but then she doesn't have to rush out the door. It is hard to hear from God during the morning rush.

That day in Gilford, I put on headphones and went for a long walk while listening to worship music. My parents live near the center of town, which was my walk's destination. I spent time reading Scripture in the town's gazebo. During all of this, I took my time. God suggested that I walk in the woods behind the elementary school. I followed his lead and went. I stopped on a bridge and was commanded to raise my hands. Earlier, I read the story from Exodus 17:8–16 when the Amalekites attacked the Israelites when I was at the pavilion.

I told God, "No, I won't raise my hands."

God said again, "Raise your hands."

I said, "No, God, anyone can walk by." (I guess you could say I was channeling my inner Moses. In Exodus 3, Moses kept saying excuses as to why God should pick someone else. I didn't want to do something that could be embarrassing.)

Well, God wouldn't accept my answer, just like with Moses. Finally, I obeyed. God showered me a vision. The vision had the map of Maine, and the revival fire was over different parts of Maine. The fire eventually engulfed Maine and then went across the rest of the country.

When I shared this vision with others, I learned that others had seen similar visions for Maine. That God is going to bring revival here and across the nation.

I finished the day with worship and intercession for Northern New England InterVarsity. Later that evening, I went to a baseball game after a nice dinner with my parents. I ended my time of prayer and rested. Prayer can be hard work trying to connect with God. It is vital to complete the time and rest. There are times that God uses my rest to speak to me.

Thoughts from that Day

The first thought I already shared is to take your time. Get a whole night's rest the night before. This way, you can be ready when you get up. Decide ahead of time if you will spend the day fasting. If not, have breakfast before coming out and plan your other meals. Don't skip a meal unless it is part of your fasting plan.

Worship is vital to prayer. The best prayer meetings I've participated in included a time of worship. Whenever I spend an extended time in prayer, I add worship. One, it helps me keep the focus on God. Two, it reminds me how great God is, and He desires me to be in his presence. The more I focus on God and his greatness, the more I focus on what God wants me to pray about.

Let me give you my thoughts on worship. Music is not required for worship. It helps me to worship, but I have had moments of worship without music. Sometimes I will read a Psalm and use that as a jumping-off point to worship. I learned this when I was on a prayer team with InterVarsity. The leader led us in a time of worship without music with a Psalm. It was amazing!

There will be a time when your mind wanders away from God and prayer. That is okay. Spending a long time focusing on the same thing takes a lot of work. Music and Scripture can help you get back on track. During that day, I finished in prayer back in my home; I used Scripture and the music I was listening to help me get back on track.

I ended my day on time. This sounds weird that I mentioned, but this is important. Prayer for a day is work. That doesn't mean that God won't speak to you after your prayer time is done. It means it is time to rest. No one would spend twenty-four hours talking to the same person. But you would spend twenty-four hours with the same person. Eventually, there isn't anything left to say, so you are just together. That evening I went to a baseball game with God. We were just together, similar to when I went to the movies with other people. We are together, but we are not talking to each other.

Scripture on Prayer

The best prayer book out there is the Bible. There are many passages I can choose that talk about prayer. This would be a very long book if I picked all of them. The ones I have chosen here will help you pray missionally. But don't stop at only what I prefer. Continue to find other passages on prayer and live those out. Also, read other books on prayer. The more you know about prayer, the better your prayer life will be and the easier it is to pray what is on God's heart.

When planning a day for prayer, reading Scripture is helpful to focus your prayer. Use these that I share to help you pray for a long time. These either give you a framework on how to pray or how to pray for others.

Persistent widow (Luke 18:1–8).

Luke explains why Jesus told this parable to the disciples before he shared the parable. Let me write what Luke 18:1 says: "Then Jesus told his disciples a parable to show them that they should always pray and not give up." Let's unpack this verse.

Jesus had something to teach them about prayer. Jesus used parables as a teaching tool; this parable is no exception. What was he teaching? Not to give up on prayer. That God is someone that wants to come through for us. This parable is about always praying and never giving up on God.

In the parable, the widow goes to the judge to get justice. Then Jesus contrasts God with this judge. The judge for the widow doesn't care about people, so he gives justice to get the woman off his back. This widow kept going to him to make sure that justice was served.

I learned from this parable that God wants us to keep going to him, and he wants to answer our prayers, especially prayers for justice and for folks to become his children. We need to ask whether we really want new disciples in our church. I believe praying for God's mission regularly will either remind you of that or change your mind toward what God wants.

Keep going to God about people being saved and for Christians to grow closer to Jesus. It is a prayer that he wants to answer. The following Scriptures help inform my prayers. They will help you.

Prayer for all occasions (Ephesians 6:18).

Paul commands us to pray in the Spirit on all occasions. What does he mean "in the Spirit"? I believe it means we need to be connected to God. That is what "in Spirit" means. John 15 is an excellent picture of what it means to stay connected. That is the passage about how Jesus is the vine and God is the gardener. Staying connected to the Spirit is done in many different ways. It is meeting with other believers, reading and studying the Bible, and finding ways to listen to the Holy Spirit.

Listening to God is part of prayer. That is done through the Bible, others, and directly. Practice allows you to hear his voice. Remember to continue reading and studying the Bible because God will never contradict it. Checking things out with a trusted friend or mentor is a good idea. While listening, you can learn ways to pray for someone you haven't thought of before.

The verse ends with always being alert and praying for God's people. Be attentive to what God might be saying to you. God will show you new ways to pray for his people to be involved with God's mission. God desires us to be mobilized, so let's pray that we will actively engage in his mission. We need our connection to God.

Prayer for a place in your heart (Nehemiah 1).

I grew up in New Hampshire and then went to the University of Maine for college, and I haven't moved back. But every time I go back to New Hampshire, even if it is just to drive through it, I get excited. There is something about returning to New Hampshire for me. This is especially true when I visit my parents, who still live in the town where I graduated high school. Gilford, New Hampshire, will always have a special place in my heart. I long for God to work there.

Nehemiah and I have something in common. Just like I long for God to work in Gilford, Nehemiah wanted Jerusalem to be what it once was. In chapter one, he lives away from the city in his heart. When Nehemiah heard how they were doing, it brought him to prayer. He fasted and shared his heart with God.

The rest of Nehemiah is how God used him to answer his prayers. The best part of this book is the combination of the spiritual, the need for prayer, and the practical, going out and getting it done. This book of the Bible was beneficial to me when I returned to the University of Maine as an InterVarsity staff. UMaine is where I became a Christian, and I hope God will always be at work there.

I pray for New Hampshire, and I pray for UMaine. Over the years, as I have lived in different towns, I have grown my heart. I pray for places where I have lived. God also has given me a heart for Japan. This happened because I spent time with God.

Leader's response to crisis with prayer (Exodus 17:8–15).

To understand this passage, we need to understand the setting. Israel has recently left Egypt, the land where they were enslaved. It has been a long journey, but there is more distance to cover than they already have traveled. The Amalekites traveled from the promised land to destroy Israel. Remember, it wasn't that long ago that Israel was enslaved people with no military training; they were tired from a long journey knowing they had many more miles to cover and facing an enemy that wanted to destroy them.

What does Moses do? He tells Joshua that he will lead the fight. Did you catch that? Moses is not going to fight. Instead, he goes up to a hill to pray with his brother Aaron, the high priest, and his friend, Hur. The word *prayer* or *pray* isn't used here, but I would be surprised if Moses didn't pray. The Book of Exodus is full of times when Moses prayed. This passage speaks to the importance of leaders praying.

At the end of the day, it was Israel who won. It was because of Moses's prayers that Israel could win. If you are a leader, remember to spend time in prayer. Pray for those you are leading and for their families. Be an example with prayer. Prayer is not something leaders will refrain from delegating but instead engage in it and lead others.

Later in the Bible, in Acts, the apostles appointed the first deacons so they could focus on the ministry of prayer and the Word. That is what Moses does here. He appoints Joshua to lead the fight so he can pray. If you are a leader, you need to spend time praying. If this means delegating some tasks, then do that. The leader needs to be the giant prayer warrior for the ministry. And Moses was doing just that.

Leaders call others to prayer (2 Chronicles 20).

I love this passage because King Jehoshaphat shows what it means to be a leader. Jehoshaphat was one of the kings of Judah that did what God wanted. You should spend time reading and studying this passage and all of Jehoshaphat's rule of Judah. He wasn't perfect, but most of what is there in the Bible are examples to follow.

Here is the scene in 2 Chronicles 20. Judah had a vast army of the Moabites and Ammonites coming to attack. And this didn't include the Meunites who joined them. At least two nations' armies were against the tiny nation of Judah, and Judah didn't have a large army. This alarmed Jehoshaphat. What does he do? He calls on the nation to fast and pray. He doesn't panic and he doesn't form a large army himself, but he calls the nation to pray.

Not only does he call the nation to pray but he also gathers them together. He realizes the importance of private and corporate prayer. Let's stop there for a moment. Jehoshaphat calls his people to pray, and then he gathers them. Let me ask you a question, you leaders out there. Do you ask your people to pray? Do you gather them for prayer? This is not only for pastors. This is for all leaders. The passage says they came from all the towns in Judah to Jerusalem to pray. Jehoshaphat leads them in prayer at the gathering.

Prayer warriors are essential, and we need them praying. We need them to come together and pray. I will add that those who don't label themselves prayer warriors must also gather with others. More importantly, our leaders, our pastors, need to love prayer as much, if not more, than the prayer warriors and lead prayer. I hope that as our leaders do that, more Christians will become prayer warriors because they will see the leaders' joy and passion for prayer. When the church is in trouble, the pastor must go to his knees and pray. The pastor should call for a fast and extraordinary time of prayer. The prayer warriors and the rest of the church will follow.

Also, the Word of God will come. In the passage, God spoke through Jahaziel. God said he was going to fight. God does speak through leaders, but leaders need to realize that sometimes he speaks through someone else. Leaders, be ready to listen to what God says in each situation. Prayer warriors, be prepared to be used by God to speak to pastors and other leaders as you pray.

Let's think about listening to God and discerning what needs to happen when someone brings a word from God that isn't reading Scripture. If a prayer warrior or someone else comes to a leader about something they have heard, test it out. Spend time praying it to God. Ask yourself if what is said resonates with you. I believe that God will confirm. I say this in light of Acts 15. Everything was discussed among everyone at the meeting. This is an essential step in listening to God.

Another essential step in listening to God is through the Bible. God will never contradict his Word, the Bible. Test what is said in Scripture. Knowing the Bible requires reading it and studying it to understand it. Writing this reminds me of what I wrote earlier about understanding God's mission. It all comes back to understanding the Holy Scriptures.

Now let's get back to the story in 2 Chronicles. As Judah went out to the battlefield, they worshipped. They worshipped because they were convinced that God was going to act. And he did act. God fought the battle for Judah; all that was left to do for Judah was to collect the spoils. Go ahead and read that sentence again. God fought the battle, and Judah only needed to collect the spoils.

This is a great example to follow. Pray, get a word from God, and then worship, knowing God will come through and repeat. That is how we are going to win. That is how more disciples for Jesus are going to be made.

Praying With Others

I have been engaged in leading prayer-based ministry for some time now. I got involved because I love to pray with others. Hearing other people pray inspires me to pray. I listen to them and understand how God works in them to pray. Then it informs me on how I'm going to pray. Usually, others pray differently than when I pray.

I encourage all my readers to find time to pray with others. This could be your church's weekly prayer meeting or extended time when you meet with your small group to pray. The nice thing is that you don't have to pray out loud. The first couple of times, you can spend it listening to others pray. While you are listening, agree with their prayers. Remember,

God can hear everyone speaking to him at once, even prayers that are not said out loud.

Some of you might say, "Dave, what about the Bible passages that speak about going into your prayer closet?" Usually, the context of that statement is when people pray to bring attention to themselves. I don't recommend praying to bring attention to yourself. When at a prayer meeting, be yourself. When praying out loud, talk like you would talk to a friend, but direct it toward God. Prayer meetings are usually inside a building, away from the crowds.

I do like prayer walking with a group of people. My recommendation when doing that is to make the group small. If it is a large group, split up and go to different places. Yes, people will notice that something is up. The key is not to make a show of it. Don't pray loudly. Talk like you would if you were out on a walk with friends.

Even at a prayer meeting inside, which is the only thing going on in the building, it is easy to draw attention to yourself. Again, remember to pray like you are talking to a friend. Don't use words that you don't usually use. God isn't looking for particular words; he wants to know what is on your heart.

Part of this is a heart issue. We need to ask ourselves why we are praying out loud. There have been times when my motive wasn't to seek God or encourage others to pray. It was more about "Look how great I am." I say this not to have you overthink about praying out loud but to be aware of this.

Praying Every Day

Yes, I mean pray every day. Those of us who are married hardly ever miss a day we don't talk to our spouse. Some days might only be a quick five-minute conversation, and it can be that way with God. I like to say, "It is not the length of the prayer that matters but to whom we are praying to." When I first became a Christian, daily prayer times were called "quiet times." I have also heard it called "devotions." It doesn't matter what you call it; we must spend time with God.

Even Jesus would spend time with his Father alone because it was his custom. He was the son of God, and if he thought he needed time with God, how much more do we? (You have primarily heard that before, but I thought it was essential to bring it up.) We are to be connected with God for his mission. This means spending time with him. Find what works for you. There are many tools to help you spend time with God.

Speaking on finding what works for you, a teenager I mentored said, "I don't understand why people struggle to spend time with God. If you love music, put Christian music on in your room and listen to it." I agreed with him and reminded him there are many ways to spend time with God.

As for praying for God's mission daily, I recommend having a list. This could be the old-fashioned list on a piece of paper or electronic accessed via computer, smart device, or both. I use both: paper, I use occasionally, and I get reminders every day on my phone of things I want to pray for. I get the reminder and pray for thirty to sixty seconds for that topic. Again, find what is going to work for you.

Closing Thoughts

Praying takes time and planning, especially when it is a long time. I know this sounds simple and obvious, but sometimes it must be stated. Pray about how you are going to pray and plan it out. Decide who you will pray for and how you plan to pray for them. Don't forget the time for worship. Worship helps you get into the presence of God, and worship in response to knowing that he is going to act. Worship doesn't need to be music. It could be reading a Psalm or reflecting on the names of God. The point is to do what will help you get into God's presence.

Don't hesitate to ask others to join you because God is there with two or more Christians. Let others know when and where you pray, especially if you are not at home or plan to have your cell phone off. These Christians are fighting for you in prayer. It is okay to have others join you either by praying at the same time with you or being with you in-person.

Repeat that plan. Evaluate the plan. If it isn't working for you, pray again to find what is most helpful. It is okay to try many different ways to pray, but don't give up. And don't give up on praying with others. The more you pray with others, the easier it will be. Suggesting different ways of praying together in your small group or prayer gathering is okay.

Chapter 5

Praying the Scriptures

Earlier in the book, I shared that I became a Christian in college. I was still Catholic at the time but sold out to Jesus. One night at work, I was collecting carriages. Collecting carriages isn't usually a prayer time for most people, but it was for me on that day. I was wrestling with the idea that the Bible is the Word of God. Some might think, "Wait, you were Christian-wrestling with the idea that the Bible was the Word of God?" Yes, I was. And I grew up Catholic and had a great foundation.

I don't remember what prompted this prayer time. And if you had asked at the time if I was praying, I would have said no. I was thinking through stuff. As I reflect on it, God was amidst my thoughts. I wish I could remember if this was when I read Billy Graham's autobiography. After all these years, the one thing I remember from that book was that even Billy Graham, at one time, wrestled if the Bible was the Word of God.

As I continued to collect carts, I thought about the mass Catholics celebrate weekly. I especially ponder that at the end of each reading, the reader will say, "The Word of the Lord," and the response is, "Thanks be to God." Growing up and to the point, I always said it because it was what everyone else thought. I desired to say it because I believed it was true.

At this point, God must have intervened because I agreed that the Bible was the Word of God. I made up my mind, and nothing was going to change that. Since then, the reading of Scripture has been a daily habit. I love reading books or hearing talks about the underlined story of the Bible. The more I understand the Bible, the more I know about God and appreciate his story of redemption.

The other thing about Scripture is that I grow closer to God every time I read it. The more I pray and move closer to God, the more I want to read the Bible and pray. I must read the Bible to be a prayer warrior for God's kingdom. All this is true for you as well. You must spend time in God's word. It doesn't matter if you desire to improve your prayer life or become more effective for the kingdom.

I'm thrilled that God intervened in my life with the Bible. I enjoy my time in the Word because I'm learning about God. Every time I read it, I'm reminded about something or learn something. It is essential to read and study it with others and God only. It is going to help you pray for God's mission.

FUELING GOD'S MISSION WITH PRAYER

What Is "Praying the Scriptures"?

Praying the Scriptures is taking the time to read a passage and then praying it back to God. Since the Bible is essentially the book about God's mission, praying through the Scriptures is a missional prayer. I have said before in this book that the more we know about God's mission, the better equipped we are to pray for his mission. This form of prayer will help us learn about God's mission.

I especially like praying through the Scripture when I'm praying for my church. It doesn't have to be for that. Using the scriptures to pray can work for anything. It is advantageous when you don't know how and what to pray for.

A good place to start is the psalms. That is the book of prayers. Pick a psalm and read it to God. Then put your own words into your prayers. From there, watch God answer your prayers. Sometimes I find myself going back to a verse over and over again as God is speaking to me. He did this recently with 1 Peter 2:9.

Reading through 1 Peter

I take my role as prayer coordinator at my church seriously, and I do this by setting aside a few hours every so often to pray for the church. One time I was praying through 1 Peter because my pastor was preaching through 1 Peter. I wanted to know what God was saying to the church. I hope this experience

I share with you will encourage you and see how this will work.

The first thing I did was make sure I had a good night's sleep. I didn't rush to get up or out the door that morning. I have found it hard to hear from God when I'm running. I wanted to be relaxed. I made sure that I spent time worshipping God. Worship is vital for prayer because I get a clear picture of God and the God I want to be engaged with.

As I read 1 Peter, I would pause and ponder God's words. I would ask him and pray for understanding. I would pray back to God about what I was learning. I don't remember much about what God spoke to me about in chapter 1, but I do with chapter 2 of 1 Peter.

The Holy Spirit stopped me at 1 Peter 2:9 and 10. Let me share the verse here:

> But you are a chosen people, a royal priesthood, a holy nation, God's special possession, that you may declare the praises of him who called you out of darkness into his wonderful light. Once, you were not a people, but now you are the people of God; once you had not received mercy, but now you have received mercy. (1 Peter 2:9–10)

I spent the rest of my time praying these verses back to God. As I prayed, the Holy Spirit impressed me that this was the church I was a part of. We have become a people, a priesthood, all for God's mission. As I prayed, God started reminding me of many New Testament verses about God's mission. I prayed those verses back for the church.

The last step in the process for me, and I highly recommend that you do, is sharing what I heard with my pastor. One of the ways that God speaks to us is through other Christians. It might not be the pastor you share with but with a trusted brother or sister in the Lord. I chose my pastor because I was praying for the church. I wanted to check what I heard to ensure it was from the Lord.

God speaks to each of us in the best way we will understand. You might have similar experiences that I had. You might not. The key is to pray into what the Holy Spirit is speaking to you. It is essential that you allow the Holy Spirit to talk to you. This time in prayer wasn't the first time the Holy Spirit stopped me, and I know it won't be the last. Whenever that happens, I stop and listen and allow the Holy Spirit to be in control.

The Lord's Prayer

I grew up Catholic and am glad I did because it gave me a great foundation. Every week I heard the Scriptures read to me. I knew that Jesus died for my sins and that confession was necessary. Then when I had CCD, or Christian Catechism Development, I learned more about Jesus and his Word. One thing I remember the most growing up Catholic was saying the Lord's prayer every week at mass, and we called it the "Our Father."

In the last couple of years, I read an article on how the Lord's prayer is an outline for prayer. In other words, Jesus was teaching the disciples how to pray. Each section has a piece of the outline of what Jesus was teaching them. I will explain more later. I have continued to ponder that ever since. It makes sense that the author of the article would say that. The prayer was a response to the request, "Teach us to pray." It is an excellent prayer and expresses how God desires us to pray.

As I ponder that prayer, I realize it is a missional prayer. Praying the prayer, either as an outline or as prayer, is praying the Scriptures. In the following paragraphs, I will go through the prayer line by line and explain the outline as I see it and how you can use it to help you pray missionally.

Our Father, who is in heaven, hallowed be your name.

Worship is essential to prayer. It allows us to open our eyes to the fullness of God. These words in the Lord's prayer remind us of who God is. When using this prayer as an outline, I spend time worshipping God. When I pray and walk by myself, I include worship music to spend time worshipping God.

Worship doesn't have to be musical. It is about adoring who God is. You can do this with words without music. I was part of a worship experience where we used one of the psalms as a jumping point to worship. I remember it as a powerful time, and everyone participated.

Maybe you do play music. You could play your instrument to worship God before sharing your heart. When he was busy, a friend told me that he spent an afternoon playing his guitar to worship instead of doing things he needed to get done. He was glad he did this because he needed the rest and to connect with God.

It doesn't matter what you use to worship as long as you worship God. Spend time worshipping whenever you are praying. The length of time doesn't matter; what matters is who you worship.

Thy kingdom come.

This part of the prayer is all about God's mission. The kingdom of God is the rule of God in people. Just like the church isn't the building but the people, the kingdom of God is not a land but people who allow God to rule their lives. Jesus is our king. The best part of this kingdom is that we have access to the King. We can go to him directly to get our orders.

Take time to pray for the lost, laborers for harvesters, missionaries, etc. There is a lot to pray for. One of my prayers for when I get to this part of the outline is to pray for my church to have baptism monthly. This includes each of the ministries that have a role in helping people come to faith in Jesus.

Remember, God's kingdom is also about the growth of current disciples. Remember to pray for your friends and family who already know Jesus. Your growth as a disciple is critical to pray for as well. Don't forget to spend time with the King and read his message to us.

Thy will be done on earth as it is in heaven.

We make choices every day. Some choices are easy, like if you want fries or onion rings with your BLT. Other choices need more thought. God wants to guide us and has a will for our life. Guide us in all our decisions and how he has wired us for his kingdom work. Daily, I pray for God's will and guidance for my prayer ministry. Whenever I decide, I ask God for wisdom and for others to pray for me.

I was recently offered a new position at work that I wanted. It would have been easy to say yes when it was offered to me. But I decided to wait at least twenty-four hours before accepting the position. I asked God for his wisdom and for others to pray for me during that time. I did accept the position.

Give us today our daily bread.

It is customary to pray before eating. Part of the prayer is thanking God for the food and for those who have prepared it. This is a crucial prayer because we need food to survive. We also have other needs as well, like shelter and clothing. And these are okay things to pray for because God wants to provide for us.

Ask God what your ministry needs to make this a missional prayer. This could be funding, and it could be supplies. To be fully engaged in a prayer ministry, I pray for the funding needed for that. I pray that God will give me inspiration for my writing. After praying, I pray again and wait on God to answer my prayers.

Don't forget to pray for God's provision in your part of the mission. Pray that God will fund the ministries at your church and the funding for missionaries worldwide. My church supports a food pantry ministry. The prayers for that ministry are the right amount of food and funding for the building.

I have friends who are involved in God's mission and lead ministries. This part of the Lord's prayer reminds me to pray that they have all they need for God's mission. This includes funding and wisdom. I want them to be guided by God in all they do for the ministry. I also pray for God to be the provider for them.

Forgive us our trespasses, and help us forgive those who have trespassed against us.

Forgiveness of sin is why Jesus went to the cross. It is also why he came and started this mission. Not only is forgiveness for God to give but also for us to give. This is all about praying for forgiveness. We have sinned and have been sinned against. I don't know about you, but I need help to forgive.

This is also about praying for good relationships. I also pray to bring people together. When I pray for this daily, it is about making friends and relationships. Sometimes, these relationships are broken because of sin. Our prayers will be about reconciliation and mending. Be ready to pray for the restoration of relationships.

Lead us not to temptation, but deliver us from evil.

There is spiritual warfare going on. This part reminds me of Ephesians 6, where Paul commanded us to put on the armor of God. The evil spiritual forces will attack us, and we will be tempted. When this happens, we need to pray that God will deliver us. I pray for spiritual warfare every day. We need to pray for Satan and demons to be blocked by God.

Conclusion

In the pages of Scripture, God has outlined his plan and explained thoroughly what his plan is. Also, God uses the Bible to invite us into his mission. Praying the Scriptures back to God is a great way to pray for his mission. The nice thing is, you can't pick the wrong passage.

Chapter 6

Spiritual Warfare

My favorite movie franchise is *Star Wars*, and it all started when I saw *Empire Strikes Back*. I loved the spiritual aspect of the movie, the war between the light and dark sides of the force. The one thing the natural world has in common with *Star Wars* is this war between good and evil. In our world, this has been going on since the beginning.

The most significant difference is that in the real world, God is more powerful than all the powers of darkness. I find the force to be cool. Who wouldn't want to lift an X-wing out of the swamp just by using your mind? Since God is all-powerful, there will be a day when evil is defeated. And that is more exciting than the force projecting myself across the universe in a world where good and evil will continue to fight for all time.

Spiritual warfare is real. Take a moment and look over your life since becoming a Christian. If we are frank with ourselves, we will see times when our sin gets in the way; people we know will not like our new selves, and then there are times when it doesn't make sense. The things at work are our flesh, the world, and spiritual forces. These seem to increase when we are engaged in God's mission and are fueling his mission with prayer.

We need to be ready to fight. Prayer is our weapon in spiritual warfare. I pray that we will be prepared to stand when it comes. This is part of missional prayer because we want God to act against spiritual darkness.

The Enemy

We first meet Satan back in the garden of Eden. He was the serpent who tempted Eve, and then Eve tempted Adam. Have you read that passage from Genesis 3? What I learned is that Satan is crafty. He knows what he is doing, and he goes for it. We see that Satan first went to Eve, but Adam didn't stop her; she sinned and offered the fruit to Adam. The passage says that he was with Eve. Paul in the New Testament always points to Adam's sin, not Eve's. Even Adam is at fault for that first sin. He chose the creation over the creator.

Verse 7 says, "The eyes of both of them were open." The verse goes on to say that "they sewed fig leaves." Do you see what is happening here? They are covering up. Adam and Eve realized that sin separated them from God.

This happened today. Satan will tempt people to sin. People lure people to sin, just like in the garden of Eden. That is a powerful alliance between Satan and the world. He is the prince of the world. Then our flesh is prone to sin. Here we have the trifecta of the dark spiritual forces that wage against us.

God created Satan, which means he is easy to defeat. All we need to do is pray, and God takes care of the rest. That is what it means to flee from Satan and run to God. As we work on our discipleship journey, we move closer to God and away from Satan. Prayer is central to this. Keep praying that you will move closer to Jesus and away from Satan.

We must get back to the idea that Satan is a created being. He was the lead angel who helped with worship. He then wanted worship for himself, and he rebelled. Satan took a third of the angels with him, and they became demons. Those demons work with him in an attempt to bring us down.

Satan might not attack you, but demons might attack you. It is the same concept as fighting. Pray, grow closer to Jesus, and flee the demons. I also suggest reading the Bible and books on God's mission and spiritual warfare.

The other two enemies are the flesh and the world and prayer is our weapon. We need help to move from the sin we crave to God's way. Keep on praying that God will help. Ask others to pray for you. Pray for the world that God will change it. I lead an organization that prays for most, if not all, of the world's issues. It is worth praying about if it is an issue dear to God's heart.

Now that we have examined the enemies, let's look at how we fight. The New and Old Testaments talk about prayer and spiritual warfare. First, let's look at the New Testament.

God's Armor

Go ahead and open your Bible to Ephesians 6:10–20. This passage by Paul expresses that the best way to fight against the spiritual forces that come against us is when we pray for God's mission and participate in God's mission. This passage is about protection and one's weapon. Let's take a close look.

The first few verses are all about being strong in the Lord. This takes prayer. We need to be willing to spend time with Jesus. How are your daily devotion or quiet times going? Let's not neglect our personal time with Jesus. These verses also remind us that our struggle is against spiritual forces and not against other people. We are charged to put on the whole armor of God. This armor is designed to protect us against the evil one and his demons.

Once we have the whole armor on, then we will be able to stand firm. One way to put on this armor is to pray about this Scripture. I will list each armor and share my suggestion on praying this scripture with you.

- Belt of truth: Ask God to show you his truth in Scripture, your life, and the world.

Take a moment or two to listen to what he has to say.
- Breastplate of righteousness: We can take the righteousness of Jesus. Ask him to place his righteousness on you.
- Gospel of peace: The Gospel brings peace. Pray for peace between yourself, God, and those you desire to become Christians.
- Shield of faith: Ask God to protect you from Satan and demons. He is our shield. Allow him to do that.
- Helmet of salvation: Praise God for your salvation and that you can't lose your salvation. Pray that others will come to know Jesus and be saved.
- Sword of the Spirit: This is the only offensive weapon. Ask God to help you understand his Word. Read and study the Bible, and live out what you learn. Satan doesn't like it when we live out God's design for us.

This passage then goes on to say, "Pray." Paul tells us to keep on praying. Then he says to pray for him. Since Paul's ministry is done, let's pray for our leaders, especially pastors. Praying for our pastors is spiritual warfare, and it is missional prayer.

Let's turn to the Old Testament.

DAVE "THE PRAYER GUY" RODERICK

Being Watchful in Prayer

I love traveling to Boston. I don't like to drive into Boston, so I usually take the bus or the train. I will bring something to read. I will put what I'm reading down when I'm close to the city to watch the skyline get closer. I don't live in Boston, but I enjoy visiting to see the buildings and see the sights.

In ancient times, you knew you were getting close to a city when you saw the wall surrounding the city. Nehemiah goes to Jerusalem to motivate those living there to repair the wall. The wall was there for protection against invading armies.

On top of the walls were watchmen. Their job was to keep watch and send out warnings if needed. An army would take the city if they didn't sound the alarm. They needed to stay awake at night and take careful watch. Of course, invasions could happen during the day.

God uses this idea of a watchman on the wall to teach us about praying for spiritual protection. We are to keep watch and report what God is telling us. It could be a warning or a blessing. Our responsibility is to watch and report. We are not responsible for how people will respond.

You must be thinking, *How does this work?* The first step is to get closer to God. We all know how to do that: spending time with him. This includes reading the Bible, talking, and listening to him. This takes time. As you get to know God, he will show you where to engage in his mission.

One thing about God that I need to share is that he speaks differently to different people. He might not give you a warning that you need to share. The goal here is to be available to listen. If you believe that you hear something, share it with humility. In other words, be willing that you might have gotten it wrong. Remember, your responsibility is to share, not get the person to do what God has spoken.

Chapter 7

Trusting God as an Act of Prayer

"Moses, my servant, is dead," is the first thing that God says to Joshua after the opening line in the Book of Joshua, "Moses is dead." Now that is a very frank start of a story. And it was this story that I looked at with other new staff with InterVarsity. I was drawn to that verse because God told Joshua that Moses was gone, and now it was his turn. Many staff with InterVarsity have gone before me; now it was my turn.

First, the past is essential. We need to study it to know how God has acted. After we know it is time to move forward, trust God in your part of the mission. When I was a student with InterVarsity at my first fall conference, the speaker said that anyone could learn from their own mistakes, but it takes a wise man to learn from another man's mistakes. He was talking about Abraham. I held on to Joshua because

Moses is more famous in the church, but Joshua is equally important.

As I said in the first paragraph, many staff had gone before me with InterVarsity. And God was telling me it was my turn. The next step for me was to act. To go to the University of Maine and continue the legacy there. Just like God told Joshua that he was with him, God showed me that he was with me. That fall, I stepped on campus, trusting God to act through me and around me.

That might not be prayer in the sense of asking him to do x, y, and z, but it was prayer in the sense that I believed God would act as I worked out my calling. It was prayer because I spoke to him in my actions. All of you must have heard that actions speak louder than words. I believe that it also works with communicating with God. That our efforts express what we believe.

Your Actions Show Trust

What does Joshua do? He sends spies into the land and leads Israel to cross the Jordan River. Joshua knew what God wanted him to do, and he did it. Joshua's actions showed that he trusted God. At every step, Joshua knew and trusted that God would show up. Toward the end of chapter 5, Joshua meets the commander of the Lord's army. This is an excellent reminder that God will be with you every step of the way.

In verse 13 of Joshua 5, it tells us how Joshua found the commander of the Lord's army. He looked up; that was all he did, and the commander shared the next steps for Joshua. Sometimes with praying, we need to look up to God to know what is next for us as an act of prayer and the next steps in ministry. Joshua looked up, and he listened to God. This could be physical, like it was for Joshua at this time (read the rest of the story because it becomes clear that God came to Joshua). Or it could be our prayer attitude that focuses on God. Joshua listened, which is the example to follow from this passage.

I encourage you to read the entire Book of Joshua. Joshua continues to act, and God continues to fulfill his promise. Throughout the book, Joshua also keeps looking up to God. God will do that for you as well. As you pray and hear from God, do what he tells you. Then as you do, trust that he will act, because God is needed for the mission's success.

A former pastor had a saying like this: "We will work like it is dependent on us, and we will pray because it is dependent upon God." I agree 100 percent with the second part of the statement. As for the first part, I understood what he was saying. It is essential to do your best for the Lord. When you pray, don't forget to act. And if you are struggling to act, then ask God to help you. If you struggle to pray, ask God to help you. Then serve and trust God to work in your life and your work in his mission.

FUELING GOD'S MISSION WITH PRAYER

The Spiritual and the Practical

Today was like every other day. I dressed, ate breakfast, spent time with Jesus, and went to work. There were moments of interacting with the practical aspects of my day and times of spiritual interaction. Both are needed for my preparation for the day. Your day-to-day tasks have a mixture of spiritual elements and practical ones. Remember to embrace both. If you need help navigating both, Nehemiah is the best example.

Nehemiah was in Babylon when the first group from Judah returned to Jerusalem. He was also the cupbearer to the king, a high position in the government. When he heard that the remnant had returned, he was troubled for them and entered into prayer because it was not a good report. Most information is about the city's condition rather than the people's spiritual condition. Nehemiah knew something: he knew that prayer was essential to the physical condition.

I love what happens next. After praying for Jerusalem, he could tell the king what he wanted to do. He prayed quickly before launching into what he wanted to do. The rest of the book is about Nehemiah leading the city to rebuild the wall. Each step of the way, Nehemiah prayed and sought after God. He knew he needed God in practical things like rebuilding the wall.

Our lives have practical and spiritual interactions. I encourage you to read and ponder everything that Nehemiah went through. Then follow the example of Nehemiah to pray while planning. Plan with God. Then work out the plan and see what God does. This is very important as you pray and engage in God's mission.

It is the same with me. I'm the Penobscot County coordinator of the Main Prayer Strategy in Maine. Some practical things I do are contact pastors, write the order of worship for the prayer gatherings, and send out emails (among many other things). Those are practical things, and I need God's help with them. The spiritual part of this ministry is trusting God to help people connect with him. As I do these things, I trust that God will act in the lives of those I'm praying with and those I'm praying for.

Planning and Prayer in God's Mission

I'm a planner. I like to know what I need to do before doing it. I use an electronic calendar to plan my time off at work, ministry activities, and fun. Then there are no nonplanners who respond to my planning of fun like a character on a Disney Channel show, "Why do you plan fun?"

Some of you, I imagine, are thinking about that verse in James that speaks to those who plan to go to this city and make money, and James calls them fools because they don't know the future. James is, of course, right in his thinking. Proverbs has a verse that speaks to man planning and God directing our steps.

Yes, I can make plans, but God will change when needed. I realize that when I'm planning.

When I plan, my first step is to pray. I ask God for his wisdom. This takes time as I wait on God. After praying, I plan. I will plan with God. In other words, I continue to pray. I pause and listen to see if God has something to say. After I finish, I will ask God if I need to change anything. As I work out my plan, I'm open to changing it if needed. Then I rest from the planning because I know God will speak to me as I relax and have fun.

The key is always to be open to change if needed. We need prayer (especially listening prayer) and wisdom. A friend likes to pray at the end of meetings, "And, Lord, if there is anything that needs changing, please help us to change it." This is a great prayer when planning with God. We might need to change directions as we are open to what God has for us. After planning for what you will do in his mission, keep praying.

Trust God

How do you trust God but act on what you hear from him? Learn the Bible and follow the principles that are there. Pray and listen for his voice. Keep praying and engaging in God's mission. I know that God will step in to change your actions when needed. If God isn't changing things, you can trust that you are where he wants you to be.

Chapter 8

Leaders in the Church

There are leaders in every organization I have been in throughout my life. I have been a leader and follower. Growing up in the boy scouts, I learned leadership skills and the importance of leadership. The best leaders don't lord it over the people. Instead, they guide, coach, and look for collaboration. These are the skills I learned in scouting and use today.

The church isn't different. I have had pastors who do a great job leading their flock into the mission of Jesus. Not only do churches have pastors, but there are also deacons, elders, and other paid or unpaid staff. Don't forget the volunteer leaders. For God's mission to be advanced, we need leaders, and we need to be leaders.

Yes, we can be leaders—leaders to help others come to Christ in our homes, church, and jobs. We don't need an official leadership title to be a leader. We only need to act like a leader by guiding and coaching. With God helping us, we can navigate the times we need to lead and the times we need to follow.

I know that there are a lot of leadership structures in churches today. Writing about praying for each of those structures could be a book. I will use the leadership structure from a church I was involved with to express my suggestions on praying for leaders to advance God's kingdom. The following paragraphs explain the system.

The deacons are the governing board. The pastor is the lead minister in the mission. Under him are directors and coordinators. Some of the directors are paid, but most are not. The directors manage each of the ministries of the church. Coordinators oversee aspects of the church that support the ministries. I was the prayer coordinator, so my job was to coordinate prayer to support the ministries of each of the teams.

You can quickly transfer the concepts I write here to other leadership structures. The key here is to pray. Leaders are targets of the enemy because if Satan can discredit one of them, the followers will be affected. It might take a while for a church to recover.

Deacons/Elders

I will never forget the first men's retreat I attended. After the sessions, I went to my room, grabbed my toothbrush, brushed my teeth, and returned to my room. I saw the pastor and the men of our church. I remember saying, "It looks like I walked into something." I expected a laugh, but I got agreement; I was walking into something.

The pastor took the next hour or so to explain his difficulties with the church's deacons. It was quite a story. Looking back, I wonder if church members took the time to pray for their deacons. In the next few years, that church went through many changes.

In the church I was part of, the deacons are elders because they lead and govern the church. The church elects them at the annual business meeting. They aim to ensure that Christ's mission is the church's focus. To do that, your church's deacons or elders need wisdom. God says in James that anyone who needs wisdom can ask God for it, and God will give it.

The first thing we should pray for is God to give wisdom to the deacons. The other thing I would pray for the deacons goes back to the story I shared at the beginning of this section. There seemed to be a power struggle between the deacons of that church and the pastor. Jesus said we shouldn't be like the Gentiles who lord it over those they lead. Human nature wants to be in control, and as Christians, we should let God be in control. This can only happen with prayer. Let's pray for elders and deacons to allow God to be in control.

Pastors

I like to think of pastors as the church's lead minister. Read that sentence again. I didn't say the only minister but the lead minister. And as the principal minister, their job is primarily to equip the saints to do the work of God's mission. This is a considerable task, as most churches have many members and only one pastor. Our pastors need creativity to do this.

The weekly sermon is one tool our pastors have to equip the saints. I see a baseball team as a good analogy for church. Everyone bats, run the bases, and plays the field (at least in the National League, the pure form of baseball before the MLB changed the rules). The sermon, in my mind, is like batting practice and base-running practice. Everyone in the church is called to participate in God's mission. It is the time given to pastor to train the entire congregation to be active in God's mission.

At other times, the sermon can help people become disciples. The prayer request here is praying for the hearts of people who need Jesus who will listen. Even this is training for the saints because the pastor leads by example. Hopefully, our pastors will encourage us to invite our friends and family to church. Pray for your pastor to speak clearly and to have the words to say.

Sometimes, the sermon is to help the believers grow in their faith and connect with God. The Bible is here for both the unbeliever and the believer. Sometimes the sermon will be geared toward one or another, but that doesn't mean it won't help the other group it is not geared toward. The key for us is to pray that our pastors will equip the saints and help others come to faith.

We are all called to pray, evangelize, and study the Bible as church members. Pastors can use the sermon to teach the saints all those things. As your pastor prepares sermons, pray he uses this time to teach the congregation in those areas. As well as other areas that I haven't told you about. The sermon is the pastor's message to the church. Let's pray that the pastor asks God what he wants to say to the church.

What about playing the field? For example, leadership needs to be done to function in its ministry. God will not call everyone to an official leadership position in the church. The pastor will need wisdom on how to develop his leaders. We need to realize that the pastor might need wisdom on who to focus on equipping the saints. There will be church members that the pastor will spend more time equipping than others. That is okay. Our prayers can help him decide who that will be.

I hope you will consider what else the church needs to function in its mission. It is the pastor's role to equip all those roles. Again, he might do it all or have others help him with that. Continuing with the analogy of the church being like a baseball team, just like the manager is responsible for developing a winning team, he has coaches to help. Pastors need others to come alongside them. These will be the ones he will most likely spend more time with.

Directors

I'm amazed that professional sports teams have good-sized coaching staff. You name something a team does to help it win, and there is a coach for it. There are the hitting, pitching, and base coaches in baseball, just to name a few. A church might have a director for evangelism, kids, teens, discipleship, a care team, and worship. There might be others I haven't seen before. Each area is crucial for developing God's mission in the local community.

Each director leads a ministry and manages it. They are required to build a team of folks who do that church ministry. In the same ways, they are under pastors to the church's pastor. They are equipping and supporting their teams. This is something that they need prayer for. Pray they will ask the right people to join their team and be influential leaders.

Some other prayer requests for directors are

- wisdom in their planning,
- training and vision casting to their teams,
- their own training and spiritual formation, and
- spiritual formation of their team.

The directors are also equipping the saints for God's mission in many ways. They need prayer to do this well. Not only that, but they are also participating in God's mission because they are ministers with the pastors, just like all of us.

Coordinators

While directors are like coaches for a baseball team, coordinators are the behind-the-scene aspects that the team needs; but the coaching staff doesn't have time to complete them. In baseball, that would be managing the clubhouse, uniforms, equipment, etc. For the church, this is technology, communication, global mission support, and prayer (in some churches, this is a ministry as well), to name a few.

The biggest thing to pray for coordinators is wisdom in all they do. They are working with each ministry to ensure they have what is needed. For example, as the prayer coordinator at my church, I help encourage and lead others in praying for all church ministries. I have built a team of prayer warriors collecting prayer requests and praying. Prayer is the fuel for the mission that God has for us. My job is to develop creative ways to help the church by praying. This is going to look different for each of the ministries. I am also a source for training in prayer as well.

I need prayer. I can get discouraged. Above all, I need wisdom on who to ask others to join me and how to equip them. I need God's help casting a vision that encourages prayer for all areas of the church. When I think of the other coordinators, they are building a team and equipping them to do the tasks God has given us.

Everyone Else

Earlier in this chapter, I mentioned how we all are leaders, even if we don't have an official title or position. We are leaders at home and in our jobs. A leader is someone with influence. We might influence our coworkers. God might call you to have an impact on your boss or your pastor to advance his mission.

The prayer here is about influence. Where do you have influence and pray into that? Pray for God to help you have an impact. Pray that you will influence areas in which God wants you to have influence.

We can also pray for our workers in our children and youth ministries, parents, and Christian business leaders. Pray that they will have godly influence. I pray that they will share the gospel in both word and deed. It might be helpful for you to list out those you know, our parents, children, workers, youth workers, and business leaders that you know. Remember, you can't be expected to pray for everyone. Make sure you pray for those God is calling you to pray for.

Leaders to Lead Prayer

Our leaders also need to be prayer leaders. When our leaders are praying, the people will be praying. The last time my church searched for a pastor, I prayed that the new pastor would lead by example in prayer. This reminds me of two passages from the Old Testament where a leader knew that prayer was important. Open your Bibles with me, and look at these two leaders. If you are a leader, I pray you will follow these two examples. I talked about these passages when I talked about praying through the Scriptures. I think it is important that we look at them again. Sometimes repetition is a great teacher.

The first place for you to turn to is Exodus 17:8–15. First, some background information. Moses and the Israelites have just left slavery. They are closer to Egypt than they are to the promised land. The Amalekites came from the promised land to destroy them. One more thing to keep in mind: Israel does not have an army at this time. It was a nation of enslaved people who had just escaped slavery. They had no military training. What does Moses do? He doesn't plan the battle. Instead, he asks Joshua, his assistant, to lead the battle. Then Moses, the high priest, Aaron, and his friend, Hur, go to the top of a mountain.

The exciting thing about this passage is the word *prayer* isn't used. I can only see the picture of Moses, Aaron, and Hur praying. Moses knew that prayer was going to win the battle for Joshua. The raised hands symbolize when prayer is engaged and when prayer is not. Moses, Aaron, and Hur quickly learned the battle was successful when Moses's hands were raised. Because they trusted in God, they made sure their hands stayed raised. It was a prayer of action, trusting God to answer and to make sure the victory happens.

I want to make a quick note about the raising of hands. The raising of hands in this story is not a prescription of what we need to do. Instead, it describes what happened and what God wants us to learn.

There are many stories after this event when hands are not raised and God still answers the prayer. Then again, sometimes raising your hands while you are praying might be helpful.

I want to discuss the following story in 2 Chronicles 20:1–30. Take a minute and read the story, then come back here for my thoughts. King Jehoshaphat learns that Moab and Ammon are coming to attack with a vast army. Jehoshaphat is considered one of the good kings. A good king in Israel doesn't have a standing army or a large one. He calls for a fast and prayer meeting. God uses this prayer meeting to speak to him and the nation of Israel. Guess what! God gives them victory. The king was faithful to prayer and God was doing his part.

I share these stories because our leaders must lead by example regarding prayer. They need to follow this example and pray and call others to pray. Prayer leaders, encourage your pastors, deacons, elders, etc. to call out times of prayer and fasting. Encourage them to fuel God's mission with prayer. Above all, encourage them to lead prayer focused on God's mission of evangelism and discipleship.

Conclusion

Leaders are essential in God's mission. They need prayers as they lead their team to show the love of Jesus and advance his kingdom. I hope these suggestions are helpful and you can adapt these to your situation.

Chapter 9

Spiritual Formation and God's Mission

I'm not an expert in spiritual formation, but I believe it is essential for all Christians. My first introduction to spiritual formation was while I worked with InterVarsity. InterVarsity required all staff to attend a spiritual formation retreat every fall and spring semester. It was the requirement that I looked forward to every semester. These were three days of Bible studies, worship, and other practices that God can use to form us. The best definition I use is, spiritual formation is what we do as Christians to allow God to develop us.

Why have a chapter in a book about missional prayer on spiritual formation? The words of my regional director with InterVarsity summed it up nicely. He spoke about the dangers of our identity being what we do and not who we are. I'm a prayer warrior not because I pray but because that is who God says I am. I pray, lead others in prayer, and teach and write about prayer because of God's calling on my life.

Spiritual formation needs to be intentional. Just like your prayer life needs a plan, so does your time with God for his formation of you need a plan. Some of you might be thinking, "Dave, I'm busy. I can't add another thing to my life. Plus, the mission is important. I can't take time away from the mission." I argue that your spiritual formation is part of the mission. If we are not right with God, it will impede our usefulness.

When I worked with InterVarsity, it was part-time and I had another part-time job. I was worried I wouldn't have time for my other duties with InterVarsity in the weeks following the retreat. I mentioned that to my boss, and he quickly said, "That is okay because these retreats are vital to our mission." Pulling back from my ministry for your spiritual development is okay. I would argue that it is imperative that you do that. It will allow you to trust God more, and when we trust God, we can rest assured that he is at work doing his part.

Let's spend time fleshing out some ways spiritual formation could work for you. What I'm going to share with you is not an exhaustive list but a list of things I do or hope to do to help God form me. Use what works for you. Research other ways you allow God to develop you. And remember, your discipleship is part of God's mission.

Rule of Life

I was introduced to rule of life during my first spiritual formation retreat with InterVarsity. Even after all these years, I still have one, even though I'm not with InterVarsity. I have found it helpful as I seek God and my place in the mission. Creating it was useful for me because it allowed me to examine my life and see where I needed to make changes. Someone once called mine rule of life a constitution of life because it was long. The length of it isn't what matters but knowing where you are going.

Spiritual formation starts with a plan, where a rule of life comes in. We all live busy lives, allowing us to plan fully, find time to spend with Jesus, and be about his kingdom's work. Your rule of life will include your time with Jesus, your missional calling, and time spent building relationships.

Each rule of life is going to look different for each person. What won't be different is the starting point, which is prayer. Many resources online can help you make a rule of life. Some of the sites have a template. Do a google search and pick the one that God leads you to.

My rule of life starts with a life purpose statement. I use that to determine each of the following sections. I review it once a month to remind me what I'm striving for and to make changes as necessary.

Spiritual Direction

During the years I worked with InterVaristy, I met monthly with a spiritual director. The funny thing with spiritual directors is, they don't direct. They actively listen, ask questions, and offer their observation. A good spiritual director will ask questions to get down deep. It is time for someone else to listen to where you are struggling to help you see where God works in your life.

Spiritual direction can also be done in a group. If you are engaging in the mission with others, you should engage in this with those people. Group spiritual direction allows participation on both sides. Sharing what God wants you to share and actively listening to others to help them hear where God is speaking to them.

Bible Study

The Bible is God's Word, so we must spend time at least reading it. Studying it goes beyond just reading but trying to understand it. The Bible reveals God's message to us and who he is. It also expresses his mission. Earlier in this book, I discussed the importance of understanding God's mission, and it begins with Bible study.

Earlier today, I was at the mission team meeting at my church. The team coordinator started with a quick devotion to help focus us. It was in the passage about how God calls us to pray for the harvesters.

Then we had a time of prayer for our missionaries before we discussed the agenda of the meeting.

Examen

Examen is simply asking two questions: Where did I see him, and where did I miss him? The examen is usually something to do at the end of the day. Find a quiet place without any distractions. Then ask God those questions. This is especially helpful after a busy day of ministry. Then pray into the areas where you need to see him more and praise him where you did see him.

The examen can also be done with others. Start by asking God to show himself clearly to the group. Then ask each other the two questions. Give everyone time to answer the first question and then answer the following question. Pray together where you need help seeing him and praise in the area.

Sabbath (Day of Rest)

Who doesn't enjoy a day off? I'm sure that workaholics have difficulty taking time off from work. We must remember that Jesus said that the Sabbath was made for man, not God. The Bible commands us to rest because we need rest, the call to rest, so we can trust God to continue the work. Because Jesus says, "Just as the Father is working, so is he working."

What do we do on our Sabbath? Anything that helps restore you. What restores you? Is it going for a hike? Or is it spending time reading? My cooperating teacher during my student teaching was restored over the weekend from teaching when he helped build things. Spend the day doing whatever restores you knowing that God is at work in the mission that he has called you to do.

Worship and time with God do restore you because God created us to need him. The Sabbath in the Old Testament included time with God and worship. This brings up the question, Does the Sabbath have to be Sunday? I say no. It is about the principle of spending time getting rest.

Take a day off and allow God to use it to form you. Then you will be ready to engage in his mission and know better how to fuel it with prayer.

Daily Quiet Time

Time with God is the most essential part of being a Christian, especially for those of us that are engaged in his mission. *Daily*, in my mind, means regular. This could be daily or five days a week or whatever is going to work for you. The critical thing is to guard your time with God and make it happen. Guard the time you choose as well. Spending time with God first thing in the morning works for me. Others, it is lunchtime or the end of the day. Find the time that works for you.

The ultimate reason for this is spending time with God. The best quiet times have worship, Bible study, listening, and praying. Worship isn't necessarily singing but adoring God. Sing a song or praise him with words, it doesn't matter. Bible study is about learning more about God, how he wants us to live, and his mission.

Listening is taking the time to hear if he has something to say to you. He might not have something to say, and that is okay. It could be about the mission, and it could be about something else. The key is to be open to what he has to say. Then speak! Telling him what is on your mind and getting clarification for what he said to you.

Retreats

Sometimes you just need to get away to hear from Jesus. A retreat is a great way to do that. I have done several retreats and conferences. Each time, I come away with something. A retreat is timeout with the goal of prayer, worshipping, and listening to God. A conference can be a retreat, but usually, a conference has other purposes as well.

If you are on a team engaged with God's mission, do it as a group. This way, you all can hear together what God is saying. Study a Scripture passage that speaks to what you are doing to proclaim the gospel or what God might say. Discuss it together so everyone will be on the same page. Above all, pray! Pray back to God what you believe you are hearing.

Retreats can be done individually as well. Look at Scripture, listen, and pray. Later, share with someone you trust what you are hearing. Before going on a retreat, ask others to pray for you. Prayer for this is important. This time is about allowing God to form you so you can be better at praying for your part of the mission and in what you do.

Worship

I love worshipping Jesus, especially with signing. There is something about worship that helps me to engage in prayer. The more I adore, the more I see God in his fullness, and that encourages me to pray. I make time for worship, both corporately and individually.

Make sure you make time to worship. Attend a weekly worship service and be creative in ways you can worship throughout the week. The psalms are great examples of worshipping God. I have also used a book that lists qualities of God to help me find ways to praise God.

Conclusion

I hope that you find this helpful. The more time you spend in spiritual formation, the better equipped you are going to be for both missional prayer and missional activity. It is God doing the work, and the work is dependent on him. Spending time allowing God to form us reminds us that it doesn't depend on us. We are invited to partner with God.

Chapter 10

The Family and God's Mission

Everyone remembers when their children are born. For me, it was the day after Christmas. My wife started labor late on Christmas Eve, and my son was born at about 4:00 p.m. on December 26 by C-section. While she was recovering, my task was to stay with my son. I was in awe of the fact that I was a dad. It was the moment that it became real to me.

I had many ups and downs being a dad over the years, and I always felt honored that God allowed me to be a dad and gave me my son. I took the lead in teaching him about God and the Bible. I prayed he would become a man after God's heart every night. David from the Bible was a great man of God because he repented of his sins, and that is my desire for my son.

My son is now twenty-two. He is working toward his goal to be an airline pilot. As I write this, he is upstairs getting ready to work his shift at the airport. Raising him with my wife has given me great joy and frustration. I'm sure that many of you can relate. And I wouldn't trade any of those moments for anything.

The Bible says, "God sets the lonely in families" (Psalm 68:6a). When he sent the Messiah, God gave him a mother and a father. The gospel speaks of Jesus having brothers and sisters. When it came time for the flood, it was a family that God chose to save in the ark. The first people on Earth were also the first parents. As you follow that first family and their line, eventually you come to Abraham and the promise of a son.

From that son, we get the story of the family of Isaac and Jacob. Eventually, it leads to David and his line to Jesus. Some of this is a recap of the story of God's plan to save the world. It speaks to the importance of the family to God's mission. Join me in looking at God's design for family as we find ways to pray for our families and others through the lens of God's mission.

God's Design (Ephesians 5:21–6:4)

God has much to say about families through Paul in Ephesians 5:21-6:4. Please open up your Bible or the Bible app on your phone or tablet and read this passage. This passage is a great place to start because it discusses husbands and wives, parents and children. As you read it, pray about what you are learning and what God wants you to learn. Once you understand what he wants you to know, it will make it easier for you to pray.

I chose to start the passage at Ephesians 5:21 because mutual submission is essential. From there, Paul speaks about the husband's leadership. What a picture it is. Husbands are to be a reflection of Christ to their wives, being willing to give their lives for her. Consider what this looks like and what changes could happen if more husbands were like this. Let's pray for this type of husband: husbands loving their wives the way Jesus loved the world.

Paul commands kids to obey their parents. He also says for Fathers not to exasperate their children. These things need to go together. The note in the NIV suggests that this verse could be translated to say parents instead of fathers. Let's pray for both dads and moms not to exasperate their children. Kids who are loved are more likely to realize that God loves them. This is another excellent prayer we can have for the family, for parents to love their kids like God loves them.

I like these verses. It reminds me that God is using the family to advance his kingdom. Kids are the next generation, and we need strong leaders in the church that will continue the mission. Those outside the church can see God at work inside the families in the church. Parents are the first teachers of their kids, and the church partners with them. Let's pray for this partnership and for parents to lead in teaching their kids.

Praying for Husbands and Fathers

I'm big into men's ministry. I was the men's ministry leader in two churches. Most visions for men's ministry that have resonated with me speak of reaching men to reach others, especially for their families. Statistics suggest that getting the man of the home increases the chances of his wife and children calling for the Lord.

That is true because God calls all husbands and fathers to be the spiritual leaders of their homes. When praying for husbands and fathers, let's start with their salvation because they can't lead spiritually if they don't connect with God. When saved, they will connect with God and be better fathers. We can pray that as we are praying for their needs. Sometimes, people need to see God working before they can trust him. I can see that with fathers.

Their salvation is also needed to be the spiritual leader of the home. It is almost impossible to lead spiritually if you don't connect with God. They need God to lead spiritually. Any husbands and fathers you know pray for their connection to God. Pray for the Holy Spirit to come into their lives. Then pray for their ability to be the leaders they need to be.

Of course, praying for their relationship with their wives is very important. It might be the most important thing to share because marriage reflects the Trinity. Genesis 3:24 says, "That is why a man leaves his father and mother and is united to his wife, and they become one flesh." Just as God is the Father, the

Son, and the Holy Spirit, three in one, so is husband and wife are two becoming one. It is this relationship that is best for kids to grow up in.

I pray for strong marriages in the church. I pray because I want others to see a piece of what God is like. It is a beautiful picture of imperfect people giving a glimpse of God. Who are the married couple that you can pray for? Pray for them to be one and pray that their marriage will be strong.

Mothers

Moms never take a day off from being a mom. Even when they are away from their kids, they think about them. As my son grew, I watched my wife be the best mom she could be. She wanted the best for him, and I do not doubt she loved him. Even now that my son is an adult, she is his biggest cheerleader.

Moms are the nurturers. When I scraped my knee growing up, I would go to my mom for comfort. And my son did the same thing. Comfort is crucial for all kids. Let's pray that moms will love and nurture their kids well. Where they fall short, let's pray that God will step in. That brings me to another prayer request: praying for moms to be connected to Jesus because they will struggle to love their kids if they are not.

Being a mom must be challenging, even if they are married. It must be more demanding for the single moms out there. They have to be both mom and dad to their kids. These moms need our prayers for strength and wisdom.

The other night at my weekly prayer meeting, we were praying to end abortion. The leader started to pray for the spirit of Joseph to give to pregnancy resource centers. He was, of course, talking of Joseph of Arimathea. When I got up, I prayed for God to raise the other type of Joseph in the New Testament—men who will come alongside single moms. Joseph didn't have to take Jesus as his son, but he did willingly and took on Mary's disgrace for being a pregnant teenager. Imagine with me how the world could change with more men like that.

Children

Psalm 127:3 says, "Children are a heritage from the Lord; offsprings are a reward from him." What a great thought. Verse 5 says, "Blessed is the man whose quiver is full of them. They will not be put to shame when the content with their opponents in court." Children are about legacy. We have heard it before that children are the future. I would also argue that children, especially teenagers, are part of our present.

When I'm prayer walking and pass a school, I pray for believing students to be bold and start Christian clubs and Bible studies. I have prayed for a teen who started a Fellowship of Christian Athletes at his high school. Other teens who love Jesus can do this if he can do it. They need prayers from adults to be bold. Let's pray for teens, but let's not forget to pray for adults that support them. Being involved in God's mission is challenging for fully mature adults. Teens still have maturing to do.

Kids under the age of thirteen can also participate in God's mission. Jesus, in the gospels, said many times not to prevent kids from coming to him. Let's pray and encourage our kids to invite their friends to Sunday school or children's church. If you are a parent, ask God if he wants them in public, Christian, or home schools. The public schools are a mission field. If your son or daughter wants to bring the Bible to school for silent reading time, don't stop them. Encourage and pray for them.

My church would have events designed for kids when I was living and attending church in Old Town, Maine. The kids' director and staff would encourage the kids to invite their friends to these events. I like this idea. The events would introduce the kids to what happens on Sunday mornings and have a little time for teaching, which was also fun. I pray that more churches do these events and get kids involved in God's mission.

We can say the same thing about youth groups. If you remember my story of coming to Christ, I was never involved in a youth group. I would have gone if a friend invited me to youth group, especially in high school. When I did help out with youth groups, I encouraged them to ask their friend from school. I have helped with youth groups that were more of an outreach than it was for church kids. I think youth groups can be for the kids growing up in church and those unchurched. I'm praying for that as well.

When I pray for kids and teens today, I pray with the future in mind. I want teens to be saved today so that adults in the future can be saved. There is one more thing I want to bring into all this since this is a chapter about praying for the family. Parents are the first teachers of their kids. They also lead prayer for their kids and encourage them in their walk with Jesus. Let's pray for parents' ministry to their kids and through kids to make a difference in the world with Jesus.

Extended Family

Don't forget the aunts, uncles, cousins, and grandparents. Each of these first needs to be saved. Keep praying for their salvation if you have extended family members that are not saved. If they are saved, they can have a role in helping our kids learn and follow Jesus. You can partner with the parents if you are an extended family member. You can pray for the salvation of your siblings and parents if needed.

Pray how you can partner with the parents of your nephew, nieces, and grandchildren. Then do what God speaks to you. If those parents need to be saved, pray for their salvation. Pray for believers to come into their lives and be those believers.

Chapter 11

The Mission in Business and With Money

I'm sitting in my living room, thinking of ways to start this chapter. All I can think of is how the public world has a lot of businesses. When I finished work, I ordered takeout from a local restaurant. As I write this, the TV is on, and my wife is watching something on her tablet. My son uses the internet upstairs, most likely to do flight simulations.

If I'm a betting man, I bet that many of the readers work for a business. Some of you work in retail or the factory that creates the products for the stores to sell. Or you're in marketing to help make the sales. Businesses are in business to make money. As people work to help their employer make a profit, their wages are taxed to support our schools and nonprofits doing services for the state, like group homes.

Places of work: businesses, nonprofits, and schools are just one more place for God's mission. And for-profit companies can fund the mission. If we are to fuel God's mission with prayer, let's pray for Christian men and women who want to do things God's way in their companies. I have a friend who owns a construction business, and he has set it to do that.

Then there is money. The Bible says that the root of all evil is the love of money. Read that sentence again. The root of all evil is not money but the love of money. Money is a tool that can be used for God's kingdom or used against God's kingdom. We need to ask, "Are we using money for God's kingdom or against it?" And where you spend your money is a testimony to where you believe that God is at work. And it shows your priorities around money.

Business Owners

I have a friend who owns a construction business. When we can, we catch up and pray for one another. His unique approach to running his business allows him to care for his employees. He constantly tells me he is not the owner but the steward because God is the owner.

My friend has the right idea. The marketplace can be a place where God's kingdom is advanced. It takes intentionality and prayer. If you are a business owner, be thinking and praying about this. I think it starts with how you care for your employees.

Let's look at the parable of the workers in the vineyards found in Matthew 20:1–16. The owner of the vineyards hire people to work in different parts of the day. At the end of the day, he pays each the same amount, a day's wage, regardless of when they started. The owner has decided to be generous. This generosity is received well by the ones who started later in the day but not those who started at the beginning. The vineyard owner tells them he has a right to be as generous as he wants.

The parable is a picture of my friend. The world thinks he is crazy to run his business like he does. The funny thing is, he is successful. Our prayers for owners will start with them becoming generous with their employees. It might look like bad business in the eyes of the world, but good business in the eyes of Jesus.

Owners' and company leaders' discipleship is an integral part of God's mission, along with the discipleship of the employees. Pray that they will spend time with Jesus regularly, that they will be active members of their church, and that they will know God's Word. I would also pray for them to share their faith with their coworkers.

Investing in the Kingdom

Jesus tells us in his Word that we shouldn't build treasure here on earth because thieves can break in and moths can destroy. Instead, we are to build up treasures in heaven. That is true today. Most of the money today is electronic, but we still have cash that we can use, and there is a way for electronic money to be stolen. There are still thieves. Just ask my wife, who had to deal with two bank robberies in her career working with a bank. In heaven, there are neither moths nor thieves.

I don't think Jesus is saying that we shouldn't be wise with our money, have bank accounts, or invest for retirement and the next generation. The principle of this teaching is to use our money for the kingdom. Investing in the kingdom will look different depending on the context and the situation. Giving our money into the kingdom is a prayer fueling God's mission. It says that we believe that God is at work in the ministry.

When I worked with InterVarsity, one of my tasks was to raise money for InterVarsity so they could pay me. I had many people who supported me financially and with prayer. I appreciate each of my financial partners and those who prayed for me. They were more than just partners; they invested in the kingdom and stored their treasures in heaven.

How many of you give to your church? I hope that it is everyone who is reading this book. When you give to your church's offering, you believe in that church's ministry. How many of you give to a missionary? If you do, you are saying the same thing about that missionary. You believe that God is working through the missionary. I want to encourage you to give toward God's mission.

The first step in all this is prayer. Just like we can't pray for all missionaries and countries worldwide, we can't give to all ministries. Ask God for wisdom and for him to guide you. The guidance could be for how much to offer and who to give to. Both are important. Remember, it is not the size of the gift that matters but the heart behind it.

Jesus gives a story about the widow giving a low amount, but it was all she could provide. It ended up being all she had. Giving is also us trusting God to provide for us. I have heard stories of individuals who keep giving to the kingdom, and God keeps giving back. Give and trust God. You could have a testimony that helps bring people into the kingdom and closer to God.

When I asked people to support my ministry with InterVarsity, I invited them to trust God. I didn't say "Give and trust God" when I asked for support, but I knew God was saying that through me. I had to trust that God was going to provide through his people. We must trust God to provide even when we give more than planned.

Businesses and Investing God's Kingdom

One of the prayers I had when I worked for InterVarsity was for businesses to come to Maine. It was a selfish prayer because I needed and wanted more financial partners. Then again, people need to work. It is how we earn money. When Christians make money, God can challenge them to give it to his kingdom to teach them to trust him. I still pray for businesses to come to Maine so people can work and fund God's kingdom.

Then there are profits. People go into business to make a profit. Profits can be used to support God's mission. Profits could be returning the money to the employees who work hard to make the business profitable or giving directly to God's kingdom. If you are a business owner, I challenge you to pray about how to use your profits for God's glory.

I have a friend who owns a business. He started it to fund a ministry that he wanted to do. I love this idea. And I pray for him to be able to do that. I have seen the fruits of it, and God is blessing the ministry and business. He has a location for ministry and funds to do what God has placed on his heart.

Supporting Employees

My wife messaged me about a ministry opportunity at a local business. The message said a local company was looking for someone to spend an hour a week checking in with the employees and being available when they needed support. On top of that, I will get a free lunch. I couldn't believe it and that this was possible for a job.

I've been supporting these employees for a little over a year now. I enjoy every moment. All I do is listen and pray for them. One of my prayers is to increase my hours to turn this very part-time into a career. The companies I currently serve desire to have their employees' support, making my role easy.

Jesus commands us to love one another. That includes those that work for us. How does that look because all employers have expectations? As employees, we need to reach those expectations. That is how the employee can love their employers. But what does it look like for employers to value their employees?

Support is an excellent word for employers. Support can be training and pay. I have often heard about having a fair wage that supports the employees to pay bills and maybe use part of what they make to advance God's kingdom. If you are an employer, please pray about what you pay your employees. Pay isn't everything, but it could help someone become a disciple because they won't be worried about money and focus on spiritual things. I know that there are budgets and plans to make a profit. People are more important than profits. I believe that if you trust God to use your business to advance his kingdom, God will provide the profits as you love your employees by paying a fair wage.

There is emotional support as well. My friend and I discussed earlier has daily meetings before his crew goes to different sites. He does that to build into his employees and let them know he is on their side. My friend also puts their mind at ease about mistakes. It is impressive when I see it in action. He wants them to grab a coffee in the middle of the day whenever needed. The best part is that they don't need to punch out for these.

My friend does a great job of loving his employees. I know enough about him that his heart is about helping others experience the grace of God and deciding to follow Jesus. If you are a business owner, pray for how you can love your employees and help them experience God when they are working.

Conclusion

Money and businesses have a role to play in God's mission. We can pray for owners, employees, and how to use our money. When we do all this, we are advancing God's kingdom. Are you praying for your boss and your subordinates? Are you investing in God's kingdom? Let's continue to pray for God's mission early and often.

Chapter 12

Praying for Government Leaders

I enjoy reading about history. Primarily, American and church history. Every age of history reminds us that government is part of the human experience. There have been various forms (monarchy, democracy, dictatorship, etc.). Everyone has an opinion about the government and the government they live under. If you don't believe it, just go on social media for about five minutes.

The Bible says a lot about the government and our role. One role is for us to pray for leaders. I heard the verse from 1 Timothy that speaks to pray for the king and all in authority many times as a young Christian. It didn't propel me to pray for our leaders. Then God brought that to my attention. I was willing to pray for one president because he leaned toward my political beliefs. Then God reminded me I wasn't ready to pray for the one who leaned the other way. It was one of those moments in which I knew I needed to repent.

Why do I bring this up in a book about praying for God's mission? Let's look at the passage from 1 Timothy 2:1–4, where Paul commands Timothy to pray for the government. I believe that this passage answers that question.

> I urge then, first of all, that petitions, prayers, intercession, and thanksgiving be made for all people—for kings and all those in authority, that we may live peaceful and quiet lives in all godliness and holiness. This is good, and pleases God our Savior, who wants all people to be saved and to come to a knowledge of the truth. (1 Timothy 2:1–4)

Let's break this down:

I Urge

Prayer is essential. Paul is a prayer warrior and a prayer leader. Most, if not all, of his letters mention prayer. Either a prayer he is making or prayers that he is encouraging us to pray. The first two words here speak of the importance of prayer. Paul wasn't suggesting prayer, and he was commanding Timothy.

God is commanding us today to pray for our leaders. If the Bible is God's Word, God is urging us to pray. Think about it. God is encouraging you to talk to him. He wants to hear what is on your heart. He wants to know what you are thinking. This is God's love for us; he wants us to spend time with him. Part of missional prayer is spending time with God because he is doing the work of his mission. Prayer is the way that reminds us that he is working through us and in us.

I urge you to pray. Pray for your friends, coworkers, and family that need Jesus. Pray for your needs and share with him your wants. He is listening and wants to provide for you. The more God works in your life, the more that not-yet believers will see God working and want to know who this God is.

It is okay to express your thoughts and opinions about elected officials. Some psalms start out with complaints to God. All these psalms end in a place of prayer and praise for God. Go ahead, complain about those politicians you don't like to God. Then allow God to change your heart toward them. He has done that with me. I still have my political leanings, but I pray for both sides of the aisle more than ever.

Petitions

Most election days, people ask us to sign petitions to request something. In Maine, it often gets something on the ballot as a referendum question. I have signed a few in my day and decided not to sign a few others. Each one of these was requesting something from the government. With these petitions, the amount of signatures is what is essential.

In the same way, we have the privilege of making our requests, our petitions, to God. Luckily, we don't have to get many signatures to convince God of our wants. We only need to make our requests. I will admit that my prayers come alive when I pray with others and I hear they agree with my prayers. In some ways, these agreements are the signatures of our petitions to God.

Just like I urge you to pray, I urge you to pray with others. Jesus says he is there when two or more are gathered in his name. Praying with others can look in many different ways. It can be done in video chat, in-person, in your home, or elsewhere. The key is spending time together in prayer. Agree with each other as you make your requests known to God.

Bring your requests to God. He wants to hear what is on your mind and what you want. While bringing your requests and petitions, don't forget the request to advance God's kingdom!

Prayers

Prayer comes in many different shapes and forms. My favorite type of prayer is prayer walking. This combines making requests and keeping an eye and ears open to what is on God's heart while you are walking. Others I know would rather sit at home and spend time with God. This could include listening or just sharing your heart with God. The idea here is to pray and to find what works for you.

What is your favorite type of prayer? I urge you to do that. It doesn't matter what kind of prayer you engage in; what matters is whom you pray to. You can do this with others and by yourself. As you continue to pray, make sure your requests focus on God's mission of making more disciples.

Intercessions

I lived in Old Town, Maine; I did, when I started writing this book. I first traveled to this general area of Maine when I checked out the University of Maine, which is in the next town over, Orono. Driving from New Hampshire, I felt like I was going to the end of the world. I went to the University of Maine because I wanted to go away to college, emphasizing the away part. The University of New Hampshire was too close.

After graduating, I did move to Southern Maine for about ten years. During that time, God developed my desire to pray, especially for other people and with others. I would prayer walk many of the streets of Sanford, Maine, with a friend over the years. Prayer is what drove me to move back to the Orono area. This time to Old Town. As I got to know this town, it was easy for me to step between God and this city. I pray for God to act on behalf of Old Town and for many people to be saved.

This is a mature prayer. This is a willingness to come between someone and God. This is intercession. It is also the willingness to take on God's judgment for those people. I think of Abraham and the city of Sodom. He stepped between God and Sodom, asking God to spare it for ten righteous people. God only found Lot and his family. The conversation that Abraham had with God is an excellent example of intercession.

I talked about my desire to intercede for places where I live. God might call, as he did to me, to intercede for where you live. He might instead call you to intercede for a people, group, or someone you know.

Thanksgiving

Growing up, my family had a tradition at Thanksgiving to go around the table and say what you are thankful for. When I became Christian, this tradition took on a whole new meaning. God wants us to give him thanks. I think it is easy for us to go straight to our requests. Just think about your prayer life if you start with thanking God. My prayer time begins with praise, focusing on who God is, and thanksgiving, focusing on what he has done.

In my mind, there are two types of thanksgivings. First is what God has done for you and others (for example, thank God for your food before eating). This could also be your job or something recent that he has provided for you. Then there are the things that God did for everyone, like sending Jesus to die for us.

I usually say what comes to my mind. Others might find it helpful to write a few things down first. The key is to offer your thanksgiving. If you pray in a group, you can always take turns mentioning thanksgiving. Here is another idea: imagine tomorrow was your last day. If that were the case, what would you thank God for?

For All People

We are now getting into the missional prayer part of this verse, "For all people." Notice what Paul doesn't say. He doesn't say pray for your neighbor or family because these are part of all people. And Paul is commanding us to pray for all people. This means we can't pick and choose who we pray for.

This is important to keep in mind. For us humans, it is easy to focus our prayer on our family and those similar to us. We need to remember that everyone needs prayer. I can make a long list of types of people who need prayer, but I will narrow it down to two: Christians and non-Christians. To make these prayers missional is to pray for their growth in the Lord for the Christians. For non-Christians, pray for them to come to faith in Jesus. This doesn't mean that we won't pray for other needs but to be on missions in our prayer—that we will focus on what God is doing.

This doesn't mean that you need to pray for everyone. If we did that, we wouldn't be reaching out, which must also happen. Ask God who it is that he wants you to pray for. I pray for the people of Old Town, Japan, and Haiti, just to name three groups. And I'm open to who else God wants me to pray for, and now I add the people of Hampden, Maine, my current hometown. Tonight my church had a prayer meeting focusing on our missionary in Cambodia. I prayed for the missionary, but I also prayed for the people of Cambodia.

Thank you for the part of "all people" you are praying for. I thank you because it is part of God's plan to pray for all people. I trust God that everyone who needs prayer, which is everyone, will have prayers. I don't have to do it all, and you don't as well. Trust God to show you whom he wants you to be praying for.

For Kings and All Those in Authority

Politically, I'm an independent that bleeds red. There have been only a few Democrats I have voted for over the years for different offices. After the election of 2016 was over, I remember praying for Trump, and then God reminded me that I didn't pray for Obama. I was violating this command because I was picked and chose who to pray for. This encounter has encouraged me to pray for President Trump, Vice President Pence, and Governor Mills of Maine. Then for Biden when he was elected.

Some of you reading this, I bet, are at the other end of the political spectrum than me. That is okay. As I study Jesus, he would have harsh words for Republicans and Democrats. Both sides need prayer in some way. They will be saved, seek God for wisdom, and make decisions not based on politics but on what is right according to his Word.

Let's not forget the local government leaders as well. I usually have to look up who my state representatives and senators are in the Maine State legislature. I would be surprised if there is a state without a website for its government. I encourage you to look them up. Don't forget the county and municipal government as well.

Peaceful and Quiet Lives

Growing up, I used to go hiking. The best part was getting to the top and having lunch. And it was peaceful, except for the mountains that had other ways to the top. It was customary to spend time on top looking at the views and eating lunch. And it was quiet, a place to sit and relax. Eventually, it was time to come down. This is a picture of peace and quiet in our lives; it might look different for you.

This is why we pray for our government leaders. Like the rest of us, they are sinful humans, and power is something that anyone can abuse. They need the power of God to help lead. It is hard to share the love of God if there isn't peace. Peaceful and quiet lives make it easier to focus on God's mission. I will continue to pray that our leaders will have wisdom from God.

Please God

During the first great awakening, there was a sermon called "Sinners in the Hands of an Angry God." I haven't read this sermon, but the title suggests God is angry with sinners. This verse speaks clearly about how we can please and make him happy. That is simply praying for our government leaders and all people.

This verse doesn't say how often and for how long. It speaks to praying for our leaders and will make God happy. Remember, this verse isn't just about government leaders. It is about praying for all people. Pray for your neighbors, the university students in your state, and anyone else that comes to mind. The point is to pray for them.

Wants All to be Saved

Nothing says God's mission than proclaiming the gospel so people can be saved. This verse reminds us that prayer is essential for God's mission because he wants all to be saved. What I mean is everyone. As we pray for leaders, it is about praying for everyone to be saved. As the earlier verse commanded us to pray for everyone, God's desire is for everyone to be saved.

Let me ask a question, do you believe that? Do you really believe that God wants everyone to be saved? I realize that not everyone will be saved. But that doesn't mean God doesn't want everyone to be saved. Let me ask another question; do you pray like God wants everyone saved? Are there people groups you won't pray for? Spend some time with God answering those questions. If there is a people group he wants you to pray for, pray for them. I believe that God will tell some people to pray for this group, and another group to pray for another group, to ensure that all people groups are covered.

Let's keep praying for people to be saved and focus on our prayer. Praying for our leaders will help people to be saved. People are open to thinking about spiritual things if they have a quiet and peaceful life.

Suggestions on How to Pray for Government Leaders

Praying for government leaders in this country can be a little overwhelming; there is the president and vice president and our senators and representatives in Congress. Here in Maine, I'm already up to four politicians to pray for regularly. Folks in California have a lot more than that. And we haven't even gotten to our governor and the state legislature. Don't forget the government on the county and municipal levels. It can add up quickly. Some might think we need to pray for all of Congress, the cabinet, state legislatures, the Supreme Court, etc.

FUELING GOD'S MISSION WITH PRAYER

The first thing to realize is the principle behind the command. The command is to pray for all people, especially those in the government. It does not say to pray for everyone. If all Christians pray, we can be sure that everyone who needs prayer will be covered. Ask God, who does he want you to be praying for? Take time to listen, and list it out.

Most people will pray for the leaders directly over them, which is excellent. If we all did that, then everyone would get the prayers needed. I'm the Penobscot County coordinator for the Main Prayer Strategy in Maine. We pray for our government leaders here in Maine at each meeting. One or two of us will pray for the governor, and others will pray for our legislatures and municipal officials. It has worked well and is a picture of what I'm talking about. Everyone prays for how God leads them.

This isn't about politics. We pray for leaders even if they are in our disagreeing party. Pray for their salvation and that they will seek God's wisdom and for God's will to work in their lives. Don't pray that they decide what you want them to do, but that they will make the decision God wants them to make. Our prayers should be about lifting them up and not tearing them down.

Remember, prayer is the fuel for God's mission, and praying for our government leaders is praying for God's mission.

Conclusion

I love the journey that God has me on. There were times when I didn't like it, but I have learned to live out what Paul says in Philippians 4:11, "I am not saying this because I don't know I am in need, for have learned to be content whatever the circumstances."

Lately, I have also been wrestling with Romans 8:28, "And we know that in all things God works for the good of those who love him, who have been called according to his purpose." Like everyone else, my life has had many ups and downs. Each one was preparing and teaching me about missional prayer.

The most important part of the Romans 8:28 verse is that last phrase, "who have been called according to his purpose." I have been called to according to his purpose. From the time I was born to this moment, I've been living his purpose. I don't doubt this. I hope that you, the reader, will remember that. Love God, Jesus, and know that you are called for his purpose. Then pass that along as you are engaged in God's mission and pray for his mission.

Let's return to the verses that have been my filter for praying:

> Then Jesus came to them and said, "All authority has been given to me. Therefore go and make disciples of all nations, baptizing them in the name of the Father and the Son and the Holy Spirit, and teaching them to obey everything I have commanded you. And surely I am with you always, the very end of the age." (Matthew 18:18–20)

> But you will receive power when the Holy Spirit comes on you; and you will be my witnesses in Jerusalem, and in all Judea and Samaria, and to the ends of the earth. (Acts 1:8)

When I was a student in InterVarsity, I asked why InterVarsity spent a lot of time training and encouraging students to be involved with evangelism when there was more to learn about the faith. I believe the answer I got was, "It is because Jesus commanded it." That staff worker is correct. The authority has been given to Jesus, who tells us to help people become disciples worldwide. I have discussed this in this book before, but it bears repeating. Discipleship is also commanded. We can't leave folks at the altar of salvation. They need to grow in their faith.

The best part of all this is, Jesus promises to be with us to the end of the age. Acts 1:8 tells us he does this through his Holy Spirit. John 15 uses the analogy of the Father as a gardener and Jesus as the vine. If we are to help people become disciples, we need to stay connected. Our discipleship is essential to this work.

Again, you think that I already wrote this. This is the heart of missional prayer. If we are to fuel God's mission with prayer, we need to pray. We must bring our concerns, worries, celebrations, needs, and anything else that might come to mind. Allow God to form you as you engage in God's mission. Pray for those you want to be saved and your ministry partners.

Let me ask a question: Do you like the journey God has you on? The Sunday school answer is yes. I don't want the Sunday school answer. Honestly, ask that question. Some of you will answer yes, and it won't be the answer to get me off your back; it will be the truth if that is the case, great. I'm praising God with you. But don't forget to pray. Be like the persistent widow found in Luke 18. Keep on praying; keep on pressing in prayer. God loves to answer prayers, and he loves hearing from his children.

If yes is the Sunday school answer and, in reality, you don't love the journey God has you on, remember Romans 8:28. Read it and read the context of the verse. God is in control. I will join you in prayer for

God to continue to work our his purposes because he foreknew and predestined. Praise God for that. This is even for those who like the journey but don't love it.

Thank you for allowing me a part of your journey with God. My prayer is that this book will help many people become disciples and grow to Christian maturity through prayer. Remember to fuel God's mission with prayer early and often.

About the Author

I love prayer! I love leading, teaching, and writing about prayer. Praying with others gives me great joy. I love to fuel God's mission with prayer. My vision is to see Christians focus their prayer on people becoming Christians and Christians growing in their faith.

I live in Hampden, Maine, with my wife, Tina, and son, David Jr. I'm the Penobscot County coordinator for the Main Prayer Strategy; prayer coordinator at the River Church in Bangor, Maine; and an avid prayer walker. I watch movies, read, and walk when I'm not praying.